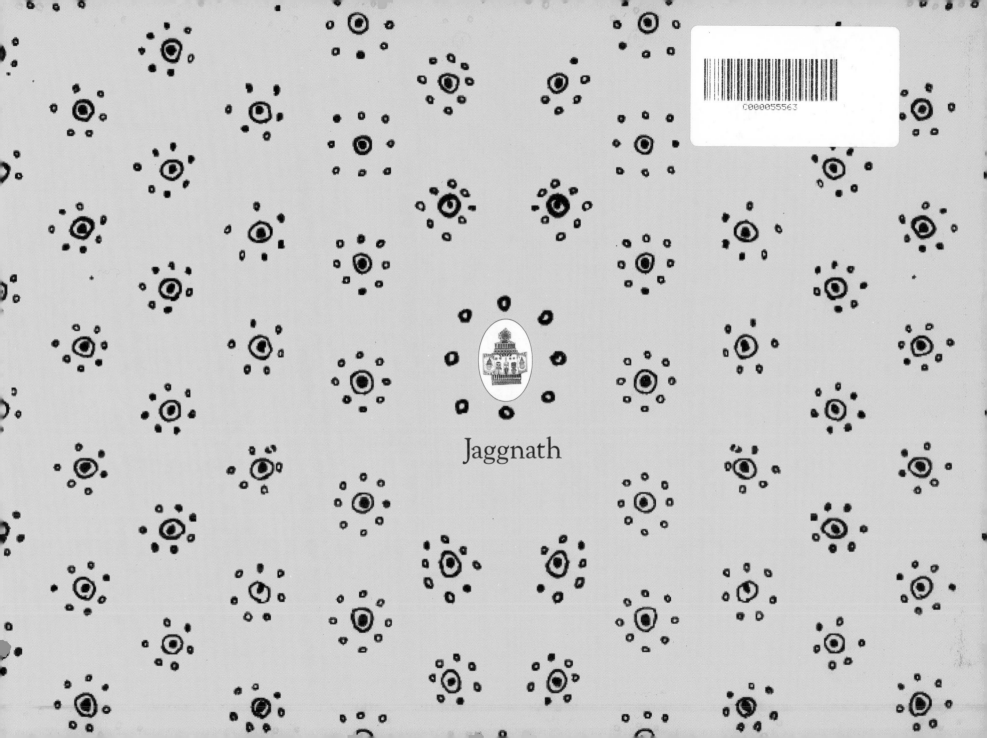

Jaggnath

Written by Mridu Shailaj Thanki

Published in the UK by Jaggnath

email: jaggnath.recipes@googlemail.com

Jaggnath

ISBN: 978-0-9564030-0-1

Illustrations by Sandra de Matos

Set in Goudy Old Style and Garamond Premier Pro

Designed in InDesign on an Apple Macintosh Pro by Calum Ross

Creative Advisor: Sushil Mangoankar

Printed and bound in Mumbai, India by

Nirman Impresse Pvt. Ltd

239, A/2, Shah & Nahar Industrial Estate, Lower Parel,

Mumbai, 400 013, India

FEASTS OF INDIA

traditional, regional & vegetarian family recipes

Mridu Shailaj Thanki
Illustrated by Sandra de Matos

Acknowledgements

This book would not have been possible without the encouragement of my family and friends, especially **Gordon Peters**, my partner, who has been consistently there coaxing, encouraging and sustaining me throughout the process but particularly through the very demanding period of finalisation of the book. I am also grateful to him for his other contributions to the book i.e. proof reading and the two poems.

I am also in debt to all the people before me who created some superb dishes that are now part of our traditional Indian cuisine - and especially those relatives and friends, not just in India but elsewhere, whose recipes and ideas I have absorbed and adapted.

However, a SPECIAL thanks goes to **Phil Tully**, my friend, who did the initial layout of the book (and would have also done the last if his other commitments had allowed him the time), and kept me going when I was getting fed-up with the process of producing a book.

Priya Thanki and **Rahul Thanki** deserve credit for their suggestions and skilful editing of the Introduction and working with me on the book. Rahul also researched for me issues around nutrition and health and Priya, as always, provided some insightful input, including the title.

I am much obliged to **Nalin Thank**i for proof-reading the book so meticulously and yet again proving that he has a true scientific mind. His clear precision has been invaluable, given my erratic style and lack of due attention to details when writing.

A BIG thanks also to my niece **Ila** and her husband **Rajneesh Rallan** for facilitating the printing process in Mumbai.

Vital to the production of the book have been **Sushil Mangoankar**, **Sandra de Matos** and **Calum Ross**. Throughout, Sandra's artistic interpretations of my ideas and Calum's creative talents as a graphic designer have given the book a form beyond my expectations. Both have displayed a surprising feel and passion for Indian folk art and Indian food. But Sushil's diligent overseeing of the artistic and creative side of the book has added greatly to the book's final shape.

And finally I owe a big thanks to all those who tasted meals cooked by me and found them enjoyable and worthy of praise.

Any mis-attributions or errors are entirely mine.

When Spirits Sag

Give me karela to cure life's jaundice,
give me bhindi to enchant the tongue,
with dals to choose from urad to moong
then stomach placated with a puff of rice.
The lassi is salty, the fruit pickle astringent;
if only I had known apples come to this
then earlier on there might have been bliss
with lingering chilli, teasing and pungent.

Punjabi khaddi and sweet and sour pumpkin
combine to make the autumn delight.
Where from? where from? someone says in Corstorphine
as the food of Diwali makes them so bright.
This meal will endure and recur from the brain
whenever the pangs of hunger obtain.

Gordon Peters

---◆---

Contents

Introduction

I am thrilled to have completed my first cookery book.

In a way this book has been 40 years in the making - since leaving India and moving to England and trying to recreate the tastes of my home for others to experience and enjoy. I can't say when my passion for food actually started but one thing I am sure of is that it started at a very early age – not that I was overtly conscious of it but the senses of taste, flavours, essence, colours and variety of foods were being neatly stacked up - stored somewhere inside my brain computer.

I love food, I love cooking food and I love feeding family and friends. Simply preparing a big meal for friends and family and sharing it with them - along with good conversation and a glass of wine - is pure joy for me. And my bliss is absolute when I know that those who have tasted my food find it very satisfying and also distinctive.

When asked for a recipe, I would always do my very best to help others to recreate dishes, but it became clear that people were reluctant to try these recipes without the security of exact measurements and precise and detailed techniques. Also, having run cookery classes in various countries I realised that people wanted recipes for not just what they had tasted or seen prepared but also the range of dishes they knew existed.

In India I had been used to following recipes by simply watching my grandmother (naniji) and mother or receiving instructions orally - these consisted of key ingredients and techniques used. All the techniques of cooking are common place in the majority of Indian kitchens and it is standard practice for recipe formulae to be based on proportions which are then simply adjusted according to how many people you are cooking for. In other words measuring ingredients, cooking time etc. are not concepts that Indian cooks generally worry about.

Being passionate about food and also well tuned into replicating varieties of food from different parts of the world without a written recipe, I never saw the need to transfer any of the 'stored data' on paper. However, the urgency to do so hit me when my cookery students as well as my own children wanted me to supply them with exact written details of their favourite dishes. Needless to say all this got me going – bit by bit old and traditional, new and innovative, all got put down on paper. However, as I love cooking, feeding and eating much more than I like writing, the book has taken decades to compose and it has finally been completed with major help, encouragement and support from family and friends.

In this volume I mainly focus on the food I grew up with in India. There are also some dishes that I learned here in Britain – mostly the Gujarati style and some that I created myself. These recipes offer an exploration of vegetarian tastes from the northern parts of India right down to the southern tip, and across from the east to west of the country. During my childhood, my family, who come from North India, moved around, so I was fortunate to encounter a variety of Indian cooking traditions from a young age. As a young girl I experienced a range of North Indian cuisines, including ones from Punjab and Uttar Pradesh plus the eastern cuisine of Orissa, where my maternal grandparents had settled. And then, when I was a teenager my parents moved to Mumbai, a most cosmopolitan city that offered the culinary delights of the whole country. My father, a food aficionado, loved to explore the different eating establishments the city had to offer. He would often take us out to experience his new discoveries.

I totally delighted in these finds, often tucked away in little by-lanes, with offerings of new (for me) and delicious foods. Then of course there was the tradition of exchanging dishes with your neighbours and sharing food at school and at work with one's friends. Almost daily one or the other neighbour would send us something they had cooked and my mum sent them her specialities in return.

Thus the world of Indian food – Sindhi, Maharashtran, Tamil, Keralan, Gujarati, Punjabi, Bangali – surrounded me and I revelled in it, learning, picking up pointers and of course enjoying the variety of tastes. To this day I cannot but marvel at the varied, and yet so distinctive, foods across India despite the use of same or similar ingredients.

There seems to be a misconception that preparing Indian food is difficult and time consuming. Perhaps it is the wondrous flavours and aromas of Indian food, the subtleties and range of dishes that leads people to assume that it must involve complex and time intensive processes, thus inhibiting them to contemplate such an undertaking. My approach in this book is to make cooking of Indian food comprehensible. Some of the dishes detailed in the book are quick and simple for everyday use and others are more complex and require time and effort but are particularly suited for special occasions and celebrations.

The book does not set out to advocate vegetarianism. But, it's still worth noting that the practice of vegetarianism and Indian cuisine in general have strong historical roots in Ayurveda (science of life) - the ancient Indian system of mind-body-spirit medicine. Also, the concept of 'ahimsa' (non-violence) has played a strong role in the development of vegetarianism in India. Around 800 BC, while on one hand the Ayurvedics were deliberating on particular properties of different food items and determining their impact on humans, Hindu scriptures were contemplating on the concept of ahimsa, asserting the belief that animals also have souls and that the act of killing them affects our own wellbeing.

Ayurveda divides foods into categories denoting their properties and suggesting that the food we eat shapes our personality, mood and mind. It puts forward the theory that certain foods make us over-active, excitable, and fiery, while some others make us heavy, inactive and lazy, and another group of foods induce purity, clarity, and a healthy calmness.

These two concepts (vegetarianism and Ayurveda) have integrally linked food to spiritual, physical and mental wellbeing. This means that nutrition, diet and health underpin all the food traditions of India. Over the centuries these two systems have helped Indians to produce a perfectly balanced vegetarian diet. All the same, not all Indians are vegetarians - around 40% of the populace follows this practice - and not all Indian food preparations are necessarily healthy.

I consider cooking as an art which has an impact on all our senses and it satisfies the most basic of all human needs: hunger. I also think that the success of Indian cuisine is mainly due to the creative ways in which Indians have, over centuries, learned to utilise almost every available food product in a variety of ways along with an astute combining of herbs and spices they employ in preparing the foods. Making use of most of the edible products that nature has provided has helped Indians not only produce a nutritionally balanced diet but also bring together the six basic tastes defined in Ayurveda (sweet, sour, bitter, hot, salty and astringent) in almost every meal, thus making it most appealing to the taste buds.

The chapters in the book are so arranged in order that before you get to the recipes you become familiar with the processes and the components that are involved in cooking an Indian meal. You will find some useful tips in the sections on **Techniques, Spices&Herbs** and **Make Your Own**, which will make the preparation of dishes easier - and perhaps more meaningful. A combination of at least one item from each of the recipe sections will give you a complete and balanced Indian meal. The last section on **Planning a Meal** provides suggestions on how well balanced meals can be organised for different occasions.

India is a country of many religions, cultures, traditions and a vast variety of natural resources. Added to that are the historical comings and goings of different groups e.g. Turks, Mughals, Persians, British. These factors have impacted on its cuisine and helped it produce an endless variety of food. This book puts forward a small - but inclusive - array from an extensive range of recipes that the country has to offer.

The colour and aroma of vegetables, pulses and spices are so very inviting and tempting. I have delighted in this and have had years of fulfilment in preparing vegetarian meals. In fact I was around 13 years old when I cooked my first full meal. My family was delighted and gave much praise and encouragement and so I just continued. I suppose part of our history is our food; it has emotional connotations. I have always been happy to share my recipes and cooking skills and thus I take pleasure in writing them down for a wider collection of food lovers, other than just my family and friends. I hope this book will make for you the preparation of Indian food a joyful and rewarding experience.

Techniques

Traditionally, in India, those who do the cooking have rarely needed to refer to books to learn the techniques of preparing Indian food. Recipes were mostly handed down orally – usually from the mother or grandmother to the daughter or grand-daughter and seldom written down.

Cooking Indian food can often appear daunting due to the sheer number of ingredients required for each dish. However, therein lies the uniqueness of Indian cuisine - all the different items put together in varying proportions create an amazing taste specific to each dish. Yet, one does not need any specific expertise to master some of the rules of Indian cuisine and produce tasty wholesome dishes. As in all other types of cuisine, it is important to have a basic understanding of the different ingredients used in cooking Indian food as well as a knowledge of the techniques applied. This will go a long way to make the experience of food preparation simpler, smoother, less time consuming and ultimately more rewarding.

Besides the usual preparation - cleaning, washing, chopping - it is essential to carefully select different spices and herbs and then decide how each ingredient is to be used: dry or fresh; whole or ground; coarse or fine; roasted or raw; and finally, to be blended together in what sequence. These procedures determine the colour, texture, aroma and taste of every Indian dish.

A variety of techniques, described in this book, are mainly derived from learning directly from my grandmother, mother and others with whom I spent time since I was a young girl. Some techniques are, however, not traditional, but developed through experimentation. I have achieved excellent results by, for example, gently frying dry ground spices in oil at the beginning of the cooking process rather than resorting to grinding and roasting whole spices; or by simply grilling a vegetable rather than deep-frying it.

COOKING TECHNIQUES

Baghaar :

Looking through the recipes in this book you will note that the process of preparing almost any dish starts by performing a technique referred to as baghaar. It is the most traditional and fundamental technique used all over India. It is also a practice exclusive to Indian cuisine and perhaps for that reason there is no equivalent English word for it. Baghaar is also referred to as tadka, chhounk, phodni, taalichal depending on the region of India in which the different dishes are being prepared. Baghaar is the method in which whole spices, such as cumin or mustard seeds, are browned in hot oil or ghee before any other ingredients can be added.

The whole spice, when roasted in hot oil, adds extra essence to the dish, further enhancing its taste and texture. Some dishes, such as dals and raitas are given a baghaar at the end of the cooking process thus introducing a fresh aroma to the dish. Some dishes require a baghaar at the start of the cooking process and another one just before the dish is served. This double baghaar infuses the food with extra flavours that make it temptingly aromatic.

Common ingredients for baghaar are asafoetida, curry leaves, cumin seeds, black mustard seeds, fennel seeds, whole dried red chillies, whole cloves, cardamom pods, cinnamon sticks, bay leaves, black peppercorns, fenugreek seeds, coriander seeds, nigella sativa and carom.

Infusing Flavours :

To ensure that the food is infused with the various flavours so that each bite reveals all the different spices used, each dish has to be:

a) cooked with particular spices, following specific steps (boiled ingredients mixed in a standard sauce is a no-no) and
b) left standing for a few hours so that the main ingredient can absorb the flavours of all the spices.

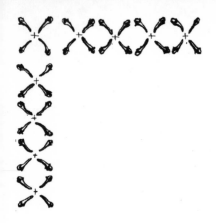
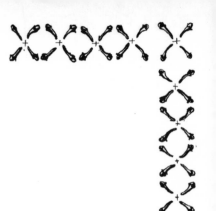

Spicing It Up! :

There are two approaches to adding spices to the main ingredients:

- Add the required spices once the main ingredient is being cooked. This method uses less amount of spice (especially coriander powder) and the food is simpler to cook, lighter to digest and with subtler flavours e.g. plain dals and vegetables.

- The other approach is to add the spices after the baghaar and if using onions, as soon as they have been fried.

  The spices, once added, require slight roasting in oil or ghee. After this the main ingredients can be mixed in. This releases the essence of the spices and enhances the flavour of the dish.

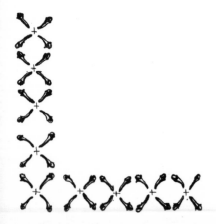
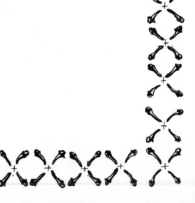

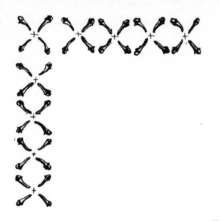
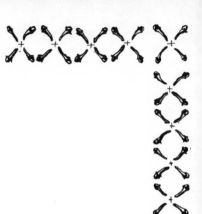

Use Of Spices:

In North Indian style of cooking, I generally use coriander and dry red chillies both coarsely ground. If I cannot find these I grind coriander seeds in an electric grinder and mix it with an off-the-shelf coriander powder in a ratio of 1 part coriander seeds to 4 parts powder and just grind chillies to the coarseness of my liking.

For other styles I use finely ground spices

- The recommended quantities of spices to be used should be treated as a basic guideline. Feel free to scale up or down the amounts according to taste, especially ingredients such as chillies and salt

- It is extremely important to know the strength of the chillies (hotness) and salt you are using. It may be safer to use slightly reduced amount of these ingredients to start with than specified in the recipes and add more as required.

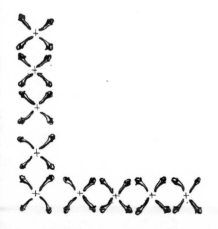
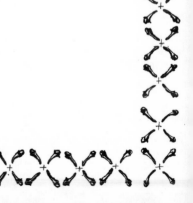

Cooking Dry Items:

For any item that is to be cooked in its dry form it is best:

- To cook it in a karahi (wok) as its shape enables use of less oil or ghee for cooking and, if needed, helps the food to turn crisp.

- Not to add salt until the food is cooked as salt draws water from the vegetables making them somewhat soggy.

- To cook the dish with the pot/wok uncovered.

Cooking Liquidy Items:

For items that need to have some liquid in them it is best:

- To cook vegetables in their own water by adding salt at the beginning and keeping the lid on the pot.

- Not to add salt when boiling dals and beans until they are cooked or else they will not soften.

- To add either coriander powder or yoghurt or cream to thicken sauces.

Preparation:

- To save time and energy soak dals for at least 1 hour and beans for 3 - 4 hours prior to boiling.

- To keep all the nutrition in and save time, where possible, do not peel vegetables.

- Size matters – cut vegetables as indicated in the recipes.

- Soak rice for 10 - 15 minutes prior to cooking. Then cook in the same water to keep the nutrients in.

- Unless utherwise specified, boil potatoes whole in their skin.

Hints for Easy Cooking:

Making cooking easier - some time and energy-saving ideas that I have learnt through experience or picked up from family and friends are as follows:

- Soak beans for 3 - 4 hours before cooking.

- Soak dals for 1 - 2 hours before cooking.

- Soak rice for 10 - 15 minutes before cooking (the rice cooks better).

- When cooking several dishes for example for a party, prepare all the dishes one after the other, using one good pot. As the first item is being cooked get the next one ready for cooking. When the first item is ready, transfer it to an oven/microwave proof dish. Use the same pot to start cooking the next dish. (This will save water for washing utensils as well as time. It will also enable you efficiently to bring the various dishes to the table when required.)

- Ingredients such as onion, garlic, ginger can be prepared well in advance for a party meal. They can be chopped as required the day(s) before cooking and kept in airtight tubs in the fridge.

- For day-to-day cooking you can keep peeled cloves of garlic, sealed in a bag, in the fridge for seven to ten days. The cloves can be chopped, made into a paste or kept whole and used when required.

- When boiling potatoes boil a few extra and when they are cold store them in the fridge (up to 3 - 4 days) and use them to make a quick snack or meal.

- It is more convenient to prepare a batch of tamarind paste and kept in the freezer for later use rather than make a little at a time.

- Chutneys can be frozen for future use.

- For making semolina dishes the semolina can be dry roasted and kept in an air tight container or bag. This ought to be used within a month.

- Use evaporated milk to reduce cooking time for dishes such as carrot halva.

With these basic techniques at your fingertips, you will find producing variations from a recipe quite easy. Most importantly there should be pleasure in cooking as well as in feeding. So delve into the world of fragrance, colour and textures unique to

vegetables, pulses and cereals; delight in the aroma and taste of herbs and spices. Make their chemistry work for you. Make cooking a pleasurable and relaxing hobby and as Indian cooks are advised, stir in love with your cooking!

Meal Components:

As with all foods, it is important that a vegetarian main meal is a balanced meal. At the same time, Ayurveda advises us that all foods have specific properties endowing them with particular tastes. In ancient India food was separated into 6 tastes: sweet, salty, sour, bitter, pungent, and astringent. These foods, it is suggested, individually and in combination have profound effect on our whole being. To achieve a nutritional balance as well as a pleasing meal, a variety of ingredients and a range of tastes and flavours are essential. Therefore include a blend of cooked and uncooked items in your menus.

- For a meal to contain all the nutrients the main meal should consist of 1 dal or beans, at least 1 vegetable, rice and/or bread, a small side salad and raita or plain yoghurt. Additionally, chutneys and pickles will help achieve the six tastes.

- Serving 2 dals or 2 bean dishes or a dal and a bean in the same meal may prove too heavy and difficult to digest.

- For any one meal, it is best not to use the same main ingredients in different dishes e.g. if the dal contains tomatoes, choose a vegetable recipe that does not require tomatoes.

Eating:

- Ensure that the environment you eat in is pleasant and appealing to all your senses.

- Eat slowly savouring every bite and eat with love.

- Do not eat when angry, depressed, bored or when not hungry.

- Do not eat immediately after any physical exertion.

Measurements:

- Exact measurements are not absolutely essential for Indian cooking. Most Indian cooks, for the majority of dishes, add ingredients on the basis of a guesstimate – a pinch here, a handful there. I grew up with measuring rice and dal: one fistful per person. The amount of water in which rice is to be cooked is measured by pouring water on to washed rice, immersing one's middle finger up to the top of rice and ensuring that the water level reached the 2nd joint of that finger (my grandmother's system). Now, with years of experience, I just pour water onto the rice and know exactly how much to add. The eyes and hands are well-tuned to measuring and guessing the amount of an ingredient required for the desired consistency and texture. With experience, anyone would be able to do the same.

- Precisely because most of the cooking is done without needing to use exact amounts, there is scope for the individual to evolve their unique approach to cooking in the context of their own or their family's particular preferences and tastes. Thus Indian food not only varies from region to region but also from one household to another.

- Flexibility, personal taste and a certain amount of daring is the name of the game. The measurements given in this book should be treated as a rough guide. They can be slightly upped or downed according to individual taste and needs (especially chillies and salt).

- All recipes have been prescribed to serve approximately 4 people. In general, it is better to prepare food in quantities that allow people to have more or larger portions if they so wish. Leftovers can always be re-hashed into a new incarnation and now with the advent of technology, they can also be frozen (except rice and potatoes) or kept in the fridge and used within 3-4 days.

- To keep things simple I have used a tea/tablespoon for amount of spices or herbs and a cup for the required quantity of lentils and cereals - a cup holding 240ml or 8 oz of liquid. Depending on the type of vegetable, I have referred to the required quantity in terms of its weight, size or number.

Utensils:

- Not many special utensils or gadgets are required for Indian cooking. However, a wok or a good size frying pan, a tawa (flat round griddle for flat bread) and pots and pans with heavy base will certainly make Indian cooking easier.

Spices & Herbs

Spices and herbs are the soul of Indian food. As well as giving the food flavour, taste, texture and colour, spices also add health value to the food. For instance some, like coriander and cumin help with digestion, while turmeric acts as an antiseptic and others like cloves help preserve food. Many of them contain vitamins, minerals and other essential elements for a nutritional diet. But more than all that, spices and herbs lend Indian cooks a hand in making endless variety of dishes while using the same main ingredients - with the blend of herb and spices bestowing the subtle difference to each preparation.

Herbs such as mint, dill, bay leaves and curry leaves are used liberally in Indian cooking and generally little distinction is drawn between herbs and spices. But, having wondered over the distinction I looked up the definitions of herbs and spices and here it is:

Herbs:

- Plants whose stem does not produce woody, persistent tissue and generally dies back at the end of each growing season (e.g. coriander, mint)

Spices:

- Various aromatic plant substances, used as seasoning for foods or beverages and as preservatives (e.g. cinnamon, cloves) *

Most herbs and spices are quite commonly utilized for various home remedies and skin care as well as for general medicinal preparations. The chart here gives some basic information on just the main herbs and spices used in the recipes in this book.

* Source http://www.thefreedictionary.com/spice

HERB/SPICE	PROPERTIES	VALUE
ASAFOETIDA	Known as heeng in North India, asafoetida is a resin, brown to almost black in colour. It has a strong pungent flavour. It counters gassiness in certain foods and also has digestive properties.	When browned in ghee or oil it gives out a very appealing aroma which then infuses itself into the food. Generally, if heeng is used in a dish, garlic is not as both have strong flavours.
BAY LEAF	The leaves are added to the food for their unique flavour. They also help as a restorative for lost appetite and colic.	The whole leaves add an appeal to the food as well as a special aroma which fills up a room. They are generally used to flavour savoury foods. Also used in garam masala preparations.
CARDAMOM (Small)	The seeds from the small green variety pods have a sweet flavour and also a slightly sweet taste. They are not only good for digestion and nausea but, I find, they also help with heart burn. The whole pods are commonly chewed as breath freshener.	It is generally used in powder form in desserts to infuse them with a sweet perfume.
CARDAMOM (Brown)	The brown variety are larger size pods with rough looking skin. They also are aromatic but slightly sharper in taste than the green pods.	Mainly used whole for flavouring savoury dishes they add a distinct bouquet to the dish.

HERB/SPICE	PROPERTIES	VALUE
CAROM (AJWAIAN)	Indians mainly use the seeds of this herb. It is a good cure for upset stomachs, flatulence, dyspepsia and acidity.	Carom's sharp and slightly bitter taste adds a robust aroma and savour to the food.
CHILLI	Chillies come in many varieties – from bright red to orange (and green when newly picked) in colour and from almost a mild sweet taste to fiery hot. Needless to say, the flavour also varies from strongly pungent to peppery sweet. Although a native of central and South America and introduced to India in the 16th century, chilli has been taken on by Indians with such passion that hardly any savoury dish (cooked or uncooked) is without it. Rich in vitamin C, chillies also stimulate appetite.	Chillies add texture, flavour and colour to food. Whole red or green chillies are used for garnish, enhancing the appearance and flavour of a dish. Chilli powder or crushed chilli used in most cooked dishes gives the food that special kick.
CINNAMON	This aromatic stick of the inner bark of a tree growing in Sri Lanka, India and south-East Asia, is a sweet smelling spice with a sharp pungent taste. High in antioxidant properties it also helps to check nausea and rheumatism.	Cinnamon sticks as well as its powder are used in savoury and sweet dishes alike, imbuing the food with a gently sweet aroma. It is liberally added to garam masala mix and also used in chai masala and toothpaste. My grandson Gethin is almost addicted to chewing cinnamon sticks. There is just no where I can hide them from him.
CLOVES	Cloves are cute looking dried stamen of the flower of clove tree with a sharp scent and taste. Clove oil or whole clove is commonly used for tooth and gum ache and used as home remedy for cough and catarrh. It is also considered a natural food preservative.	Cloves are used in both savoury and sweet preparations adding a tempting fragrance to the food. Cloves are also utilised in garam masala, chai masala and toothpaste.

HERB/SPICE	PROPERTIES	VALUE
CORIANDER	A highly aromatic herb, coriander is used in vary many forms. However, use of its whole seeds, powder and fresh leaves are the most common. Coriander is considered good for the digestion.	Coriander livens up any savoury dish with its distinct aroma and enhances its taste and texture. In right quantity its powder can be used as a thickener. Fresh leaves add extra colour and bouquet to food.
CUMIN SEEDS	Cumin has a sharp but pleasant aroma. When fried or roasted its fragrance can fill up a room. The seeds are used in most Baghaars. It aids digestion and is used in many a concoction for this purpose.	Cumin baghaar adds a very special flavour to food. Cumin powder is commonly used to flavour Gujarati food enhancing its aroma, texture and taste.
CURRY LEAVE	The fresh leaves have a very distinct and pleasing flavour. Rich in essential oils, the fresh leaves also contain vitamin A & calcium.	Curry leaves are used copiously in seasoning South Indian and Western Indian foods adding a fresh fragrance to the dishes. They are also blended with other ingredients to make chutneys.
FENNEL	Fennel is sweet and sharp both in taste and flavour. It has carminative qualities and helps digestion. It is also used as a mouth freshener.	Both the fennel seeds and powder are used mainly in the cuisine of Bengal and Kashmir giving it a distinguished taste. In North India it is used in certain sweets for its flavour and particular properties.
FENUGREEK SEEDS	Fenugreek seeds have a bitter flavour and taste. Fenugreek can help with bronchitis, coughs, respiratory problems, diabetes and sinus conditions. It is also good for increasing milk in nursing mothers. Its green leaves are high in iron.	When cooked the fenugreek seeds lose some of the bitterness but its bitter flavour infused in food gives the dish a very special bouquet. Vegetable cooked with its leaves can be bitter in taste but rich in minerals. Powdered seeds mixed with yoghurt are used as hair conditioner in some parts of India.

HERB/SPICE	PROPERTIES	VALUE
GARLIC	The herb used worldwide is considered to have very many preventative and curative properties. It is shown to be highly antiseptic and helps in building resistance to infection. It is used as a remedy for common colds and coughs, indigestion and much more. Raw garlic has a very strong and pungent taste and odour.	**Fried in butter or oil, garlic releases the most irresistible fragrance and imbues the food with it. Many find the taste & flavour of garlic too strong and lingering on breath.**
GARAM MASALA	Garam Masala, (a mixture of spices like cloves, bayleaf, cardamom - large and small - cinnamon sticks, nutmeg, dry ginger and coriander seeds) basically means 'hot spice'. In India it can vary from region to region (also household to household). The amount of spices decided is dependent on which ones are favoured. It carries with it all the properties of the individual spices.	**Needless to say, with such a mix of spices, garam masala bouquet is incomparable.**
GINGER	Ginger is a root spice with a sweet hot taste and fragrance. In home remedies it is most commonly used for coughs and colds. It also has carminative properties.	**Ginger is used in savoury as well as sweet dishes adding a very distinct taste and flavour to the food.**
MINT	Mint, in Indian cooking is valued for its fresh fragrance and its leaves are mainly used for making chutneys. It is a herb much used in Ayruvedic medicine and in home remedies, generally used to aid digestion.	**Mint chutneys – sweet or sour – besides being delicious, fill up a room with a most enticing and refreshing aroma**

HERB/SPICE	PROPERTIES	VALUE
MUSTARD SEEDS	Mustard seeds are more in use in South Indian, Bengali and Western Indian cooking. Their aroma only becomes noticeable when cooked or ground. The seeds are full of fatty oil (30%).	When popped in oil the seeds give out a hot and spicy flavour which then permeates the food.
PANCH PHODONI (FIVE BAGHAAR SEEDS)	This mixture of seeds consists of cumin, fennel, fenugreek, kalonji (nigella sativa) and mustard. It is generally used in pickle preparations and certain baghaars.	As Panch Phodoni is a combination of 5 flavours brought together, its bouquet in any dish simply fills the nostrils and is very pleasing to the palate.
TANDOORI MASALA	Tandoori masala is a blend of Kashmiri chilli (slightly hot & sweet), ground fenugreek, cumin & coriander seeds; garlic, ginger, clove, nutmeg, mace, pepper, clove, black cardamom and cinnamon powder; and red food colouring.	The masala adds a most mouth watering colour and aroma to the food.
TURMERIC	Fresh turmeric comes in nodules (bit like ginger), dried and then ground into powder. It can vary in colour from bright yellow to verging on orange. It is used in cooking, medicine and cosmetic for its anti-inflammatory, antiseptic, anti-bacterial and many other properties.	Turmeric gives food an appealing colour and distinct flavour.

USING HERBS AND SPICES

The adding-in of herbs and spices in Indian food is well thought through and planned on the bases of the properties of both the main ingredients and the herbs and spices. The condiments not only have to complement the main body of the food but also balance out or counteract its negative properties. For instance dals and beans are heavy to digest and thus are always cooked with cumin and coriander; to offset the gassiness produced by cauliflower it is cooked with ginger.

As many food aficionados have said, using fresh herbs and grinding spices just before cooking a dish truly enhances the taste and flavour of food. However, our way of life today does not leave us time for such thoroughness. Of course, with an electric mixer-grinder one could grind some of the spices at home.

Nevertheless, most of the ground spices available in the shops today are of good quality, packed for long shelf life, thus maintaining their flavours and properties. Using these one can still achieve very satisfactory results. Also, one can, with some mixing and blending, get the quality and texture to ones liking. For instance, for some dishes I prefer to use coarsely ground coriander or use chilli powder which will add colour as well as pungency. To save myself time and effort I simply grind a certain amount of coriander seeds and mix this in with the shop bought powder thus giving it a rough texture or instead of buying 'Degi Mirch' (chilli of Kashmiri origin) specially, I mix half and half of chilli and paprika powders and get the result I want.

With the measurement guidelines in this book and with experience you will discover the magic of spices and blend them to your own and family's liking – a little bit less here, a bit more there and voila! A perfect outcome!

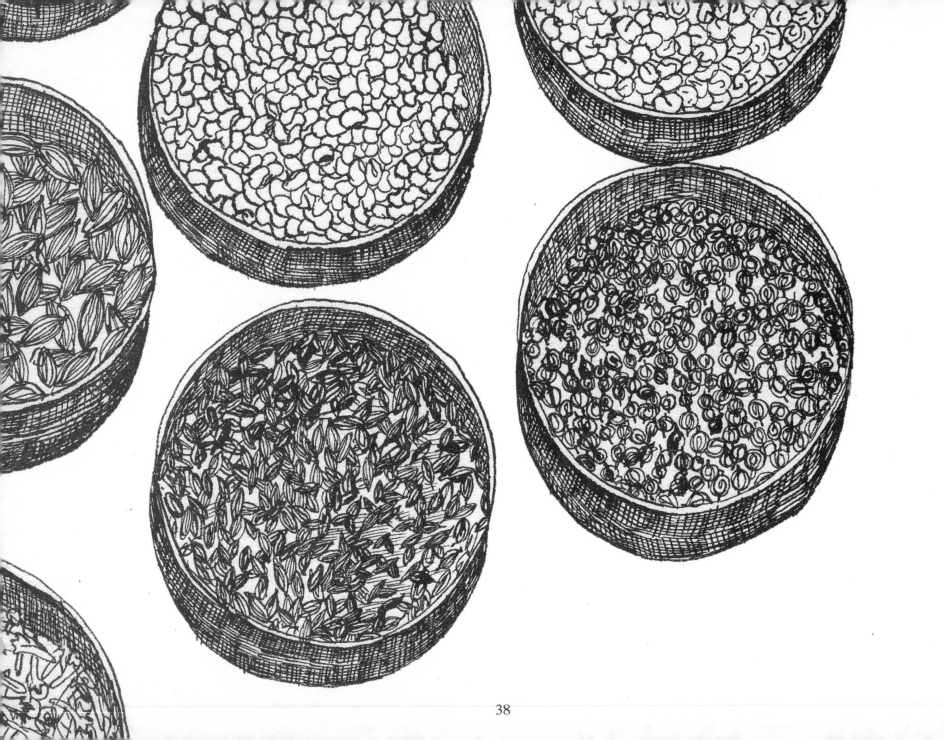

Other

OIL The type of oil used for cooking is very dependent on the region and what is grown there. For example, while in South India coconut oil is in common use, in Gujarat peanut and sesame oils are used for everyday cooking. In Orissa, Bengal and Punjab people are keen on using mustard oil.

All oils have their particular flavours and properties and add specific taste and aroma to the food.

In general, I am happy to use sunflower oil for most of my cooking. For deep frying I tend to use vegetable oil and for dry dishes I prefer to use mustard oil. This thick, bright yellow oil has a sharp, pungent smell and taste and precisely for that reason I like it. Mustard oil is said to improve circulation and strengthen bones. Thus babies (and adults) are massaged with this oil vigorously.

GHEE The best ghee is a home made one but often it is not worth going through the bother if you are not going to use it regularly. Of course once made it can be kept in air tight container for at least a year.

BUTTER If using butter (as a substitute for ghee), I tend to favour the unsalted variety. For sweet dishes, needless to say, only unsalted butter will do.

(I feel it is better for health to use small amounts of natural ingredients such as butter and cream rather than processed items such as margarine or substitute cream)

SOURING AGENTS In North Indian food mainly lemon is used to add tanginess to the dishes and in South Indian food it is mainly tamarind with less of lemon.

However, for certain kinds of dishes North Indians also use amchoor (raw, dried mango powder), pomegranate seeds and tamarind.

Make Your Own

I find that some shop-bought items are a poor substitute for home-made of the same, especially ingredients such as ghee, yoghurt etc. Of course, the other problem is that not all required ingredients for the preparation of a dish are available everywhere. Hence, detailed in this section are the techniques for some of the items that can easily be made at home.

GHEE Making ghee at home is not only easy but also rewarding as the quality is guaranteed. Also, while in the making, its fragrance fills up the kitchen, which I find very pleasant. As ghee can be stored for at least a year in glass jar or steel container one can make a substantial quantity. However, one 250 gram packet of butter will give you approximately 1½ cup of ghee.

For a better quality it is best to use unsalted butter.

Place preferred amount of butter in a good size pan and leave it on low heat to melt and bubble till the liquid turns golden brown (the time will depend on the amount). Leave it to cool and once cold strain the ghee in a clean, dry air-tight container. Store it in a cool place. The liquid will solidify and can be used as and when required.

My grandfather was an excellent judge of good ghee. When the village vendors came to sell ghee, my grandfather would be summoned to test its quality. This he would do not by tasting but by rubbing a small quantity on the back of his hand and taking in the aroma. Only on his say so would my grandmother make the purchase.

YOGHURT Home made yoghurt is absolutely yummy and full of all the good bacteria for which yoghurt is so valued. To get a good result one needs a warm place. Also, you will need at least a spoon full of live yoghurt as the starting culture. I prefer making yoghurt with whole milk because it sets better – in fact for really thick-set yoghurt, once the milk has boiled I simmer it until at least a quarter has evaporated (or add ½ a cup up cream). If you do not like the skin that forms on the milk and the yoghurt remove it and use it to make butter.

Boil the required amount of milk of choice. Let it cool till its temperature is just above warm (finger test: when you dip your finger in it, it feels hot but not burning hot). Transfer the milk in container you want to set the yoghurt in and mix in the culture (1½ tablespoon culture per ½ litre of milk). Put a lid on the container, wrap it with a thick cloth and place it in warm area of the house, e.g. airing cupboard (especially in winter), for at least 8 hours. Once you have tried the home made version of yoghurt, you may never want to return to the commercial variety.

SPROUTED MOONG It is suggested that sprouted beans, grains and seeds are easier to digest. Once sprouted they also increase in nutritional value. They take a shorter time to cook and acquire a nutty chewy taste.

Wash 1 cup of moong beans and leave them soaking for 4-5 hours. Remove from water and spread these on a tray or a colander, sprinkle some warm water over them and cover with wet tea towel. Leave them to germinate in a warm area of the house for approximately 24 hours. Dampen the tea towel from time to time. The end result should be about 2 ½ cups of nicely sprouted beans ready for use raw or for cooking.

Similar method can be adopted for germinating most other beans and seeds.

GARAM MASALA In India the ingredients for garam masala vary from region to region. Besides, depending on the household's taste one ingredient can be more dominant than others, e.g. if one prefers sweeter smelling masala then cardamom can be the chief amongst all other. Another advantage of making garam masala at home is that the freshness of its aroma is beyond compare. Also one can make it into a powder or keep it slightly rough which adds that special texture and taste to the food.

Collect a mixture of spices: (1 tablespoon each) cloves, cardamom seeds, dry ginger powder, coriander seeds, cumin seeds; ½ tablespoon black peppercorns, 3 bay-leaves, ½ nutmeg, 3 small cinnamon sticks. Except the ginger, roast all other ingredients on very gentle heat for 5 to 7 minutes. When absolutely cold grind them to a consistency of your preference. Store in clean dry jar and keep in a cool place.

For a sweeter smelling masala, use small green cardamom and extra nutmeg. For a hotter masala, use slightly larger amount of peppercorns, ginger and cloves.

PANEER Paneer is one of the most versatile milk products and can be turned into sweet or savoury dish. Many supermarkets now stock it in their cheese section but it can be bought from any South Asian store. However, the store variety is a bit less succulent as opposed to the home-made version.

One litre of milk will give you roughly 1 cup of paneer.

Bring to boil a litre of whole milk. At the point of boiling add a tablespoon of lemon juice or vinegar. The milk will split into paneer and water. Keep this simmering for a few minutes. If the mixture remains milky add more lemon juice or vinegar (teaspoon at a time) till the water turns clear blue (if too much tart element is added at the start you end up with a soft mush for paneer). Take it off the heat and drain the water through a muslin cloth or a sieve with a strong tissue paper placed in it. Tie up the cloth and hang for a few hours (or overnight) OR wrap the paneer in the tissue, place it on a flat surface, put some weight on it (to squeeze out the water) and leave for few hours. Use as desired, including for making sandwiches.

Paneer has less fat content than ordinary cheeses and is lighter than milk to digest.

Starters & Snacks

There is no tradition of serving starters with Indian meals. While many of the snacks mentioned here may be offered as an accompaniment with drinks, most Indians, including myself, still go straight for the main meal. However, snacks are something we are happy to have at any time of the day - and in India they are so easily available everywhere. There, every street, even in small towns, will have at least one cafe or kiosk offering the most tempting fare. And then there are the pushcart-walas, bringing enticing goodies almost to your doorstep, so persuasive in their call and description of the offerings.

For this book I have put together a selection (they also happen to be my favourite) from the different places in India I have lived in or visited.

RAW BANANA CUTLETS

Cooking time:
30 minutes

3 raw bananas (boiled and mashed)
¼ cup peanuts (coarsely ground)
1 small onion (finely chopped)
¼ cup semolina
¾ teaspoon salt
1 green chilli
½ cup green coriander leaves (chopped)
½ inch ginger
1 pod garlic

OIL FOR FRYING

Grind the garlic, chilli and ginger into a rough paste. Sauté the onion in a little oil till pink.

Blend these and all the other ingredients together and make roughly 16 to 20 balls. Flatten them and deep fry in hot oil on both sides till golden.

Serve hot with coconut chutney 3 (pg 245)

This is a very popular dish in South India.

ACHARI ALOO

Cooking time:
15 minutes

4 medium potatoes
(boiled in skin, peeled and chop in bite size chunks)
4 tablespoons mustard oil
(use olive oil if mustard oil not available)
2 teaspoons granulated mustard
½ teaspoon salt
2 green chillies sliced in 4 lengthways
¼ cup green coriander leaves (chopped)

In a shallow pan, heat 2 tablespoons of oil and cook the potatoes in the oil on low heat for 1 to 2 minutes. Add the salt and toss the potatoes around leaving them on low heat for another minute or two. Turn off the heat. Mix in the remaining oil and mustard. Garnish with coriander and green chillies before serving. This can be served cold or hot.

A few years ago, on a trip to Nepal, we stayed in a really nice hotel in Pokhara with our room overlooking the lake. We used to sit out by the lake for hours watching the bird, animal and human activities - all very purposeful and interesting. The food was nice enough but, overall, on offer were the usual dishes found on Indian restaurant menus universally. However, this potato dish, actually made with oil from pickle and its masala, was something I had never eaten before. It was just so delicious with a tangy taste and a sharp flavour that I decided to adapt it so as it could be made even if one did not have pickle oil. Hence this recipe - it tastes less intense than when made without pickle oil but still great.

PAKORAS
(Potatoes/ Cauliflower / Aubergine/ Bread)

Cooking time:
40 - 50 minutes

2 large potatoes (peeled and sliced – very thin rounds)
OR
1 medium cauliflower (chopped into bite size pieces)
OR
2 medium aubergines (cut into thin round slices)
OR
6 medium slices of white bread (cut into halves or triangles)

Batter

1½ cup gram flower
2 green chillies (finely chopped)
¼ cup green coriander leaves (chopped)
1 tablespoon crushed coriander seed
OR 1 teaspoon of kalonji
garlic paste (optional)
1 teaspoon salt
2 tablespoons oil
2 tablespoons lemon juice
water

OIL FOR FRYING

Mix all the batter ingredients and add the water gently to make a batter slightly thinner than a thick soup consistency. Dip slices of the chosen vegetable into the batter and deep fry in hot oil on both sides till golden brown. Serve with chutney of choice.

The pakoras can be fried earlier and put under a hot grill or oven for a few minutes before serving.

Garlic can be substituted with 1 medium onion (finely chopped)

A mixed platter can be produced by using smaller amount of vegetables.

For comfort and cheer on a cold rainy day, nothing serves better than freshly made pakoras with chutney and hot chai (pg 252).

ONION PAKORAS

Cooking time:
30 - 40 minutes

1½ cup gram flour
3 large onions (peeled and chopped - thin long pieces)
1-2 green chillies (finely chopped)
¼ cup green coriander leaves (chopped)
1 tablespoon crushed coriander seed
1 teaspoon salt
2 tablespoons oil
2 tablespoons lemon juice
water

OIL FOR FRYING

Rub the salt into the onions and let them sit for at least an hour. Mix all ingredients into the onions. The onions should have given out enough liquid to make a loose mix. If the mix is too dry add spoonfuls of water at a time to make a loose, dryish mix. Using fingers, carefully drop small amounts of the mixture into hot oil and fry till golden brown. Serve with chutney of choice.

Unlike the other pakoras, where you can sit the batter, these have to be fried as soon as the mix is done. Only then do they come out crinkly and really crispy. While they can be fried earlier and put under a hot grill for a few minutes before serving, they are at their best when served fresh.

These pakoras are a Mumbai speciality, no shape but a real crunch to them.

MOONG DAL BHAJIAS

Cooking time:
30 - 40 minutes

1 cup mung dal
(soaked for at least 2 hours and ground into a thick paste)
1 medium onion (finely chopped)
2 green chillies (finely chopped)
OR teaspoon of black pepper (roughly crushed)
¼ cup green coriander leaves (chopped)
1 teapoon salt
2 tablespoons oil

OIL FOR FRYING

Mix all the ingredients. Using a spoon or hand, drop small dollops of mixture into the hot oil and fry on both sides till golden brown. Serve with chutney of choice.

This dish can be fried earlier and put under a hot grill for few minutes before serving.

This dish can be made with blackeyed beans (they come out more fluffy and lighter).

The memories of this go back to eating these with my sisters at street food stalls on Juhu beach in Mumbai. They were floating in a sweet-sour tamarind chutney, topped with a dollop of yoghurt, sprinkled with crushed chilli and sweet mint chutney. What a mix! This was one dish among many other mouth watering snacks, such as Pani Puri. The round crispy balls (puri) were filled deftly, one at a time, with sweet and sour chutneys and tangy, spicy tamarind water (pani) and swiftly served by 'bhaiya' (brother) – the vendor.

MIXED VEGETABLE PAKORAS

Cooking time:
30 - 40 minutes

1½ cup gram flour
1 medium onion (peeled and chopped into small pieces)
1 medium potato (peeled and chopped into small pieces)
1 cup spinach (roughly chopped)
OR cauliflower (chopped fine)
2 green chillies (finely chopped)
¼ cup green coriander leaves (chopped)
1 tablespoon crushed coriander seeds
OR 1 teaspoon of kalonji
1 teaspoon salt
2 tablespoons oil
2 tablespoons lemon juice
¼ cup water

OIL FOR FRYING

Mix all the ingredients and add the water gently to make a thick paste. Using a spoon or fingers drop small dollops of the mixture into hot oil and fry on both sides till golden brown. Serve with chutney of choice.

The pakoras can be fried earlier and put under a hot grill for few minutes before serving.

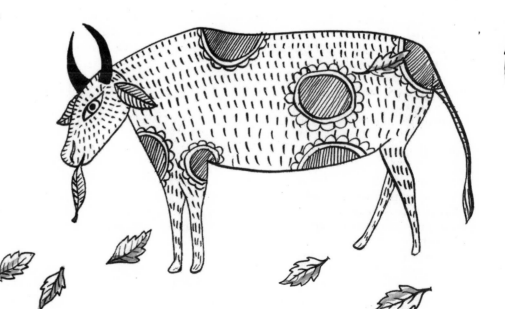

HAANDVO

Cooking time:
75 - 85 minutes

Base

1 cup gram flour
1 cup rice flour
1 cup yoghurt (sour)
½ cup oil
1 tablespoon of garlic paste
1 tablespoon of green chilli paste
1 tablespoon of ginger paste
1¼ teaspoon salt
1 tablespoon sugar

Additional

¼ cup of green peas
¼ cup of finely chopped cabbage
¼ cup of finely chopped onions
¼ cup of grated carrots
¼ cup of green coriander leaves (chopped)

For Baghaar

4 tablespoons oil
2 tablespoons of sesame seeds
OR desiccated coconut
1 tea spoon of mustard seeds
6-8 curry leaves
2 green or red chillies (whole)

Mix all the base ingredients in a large bowl and leave in a warm place for at least 8 hours before cooking time.

Turn oven on to a medium heat. Mix in the additional ingredients to the base mixture. Oil a deep, square, oven proof, dish (size:28 cm) and pour in the mixture. Cook in the oven until the top is nicely browned (approximately 45 minutes).

Baghaar: Heat the oil in a small pan and add mustard seeds. As soon as they pop, add all the other baghaar ingredients. Spread on top of the baked haandvo. Leave for 10 to 15 minutes to cool, cut into squares and serve with coconut chutney 2 (pg 245).

Haandvo pieces, with chutney and a bit of salad, can serve as a meal by themselve because all the necessary nutrition is contained within the dish. The number of ingredients make it seem a very complex recipe but, because it is oven baked, once you have put all the bits together, it is an easy snack to make.

ALOO CHOP

Cooking time:
45 - 50 minutes

Filling

6 medium size potatoes (boiled, peeled and chopped fine)
2 medium onions (chopped into thin 2cm slices)
1 tablespoon crushed garlic
2 tablespoons crushed ginger
2 tablespoons coriander powder
1 teaspoon crushed chilli
¼ teaspoon turmeric
1 teaspoon salt
½ teaspoon cumin seed
6 tablespoons of oil

Batter

1½ cup gram flour
½ teaspoon salt
½ teaspoon soda bicarbonate

OIL FOR FRYING

Heat the 6 tablespoons of oil in a good size wok or frying pan. Drop the cumin seeds in the oil and as soon as they brown, add onions. Nicely brown the onions and add ginger and garlic. Toss a few times, add in all the spices and stir for 15 seconds.

Add the potatoes and leave cooking for at least 15 minutes on very low heat, stirring the mixture from time to time. Leave the potatoes to cool. When mixture is cool, divide it into 10 to 12 portions and roll each into a round flat shape.

Together with a spoon of oil, mix the batter ingredients to a thick soup consistency. Dip the potato chops in the batter and fry on both sides in hot oil till golden. Serve hot with sour mint chutney (pg 243) and sweet tamarind (pg 248).

The aloo chop can be fried earlier and put under a hot grill for a few minutes before serving.

Once, when travelling with Manju, my older sister, to visit our grandmother in Baripada, we had to wait in a small town for our connecting bus. Rather than hang around at the bus stop we made ourselves comfortable in a roadside tea shop and ordered chai and aloo chops. Both Manju and I agreed that these were the best aloo chops we had ever had. We never forgot, sitting in this one horse (perhaps one rickshaw would be more accurate) town, chatting and enjoying our hot, spicy snack and chai, too busy to worry about how very conspicuous we must have been - two young women on their own.

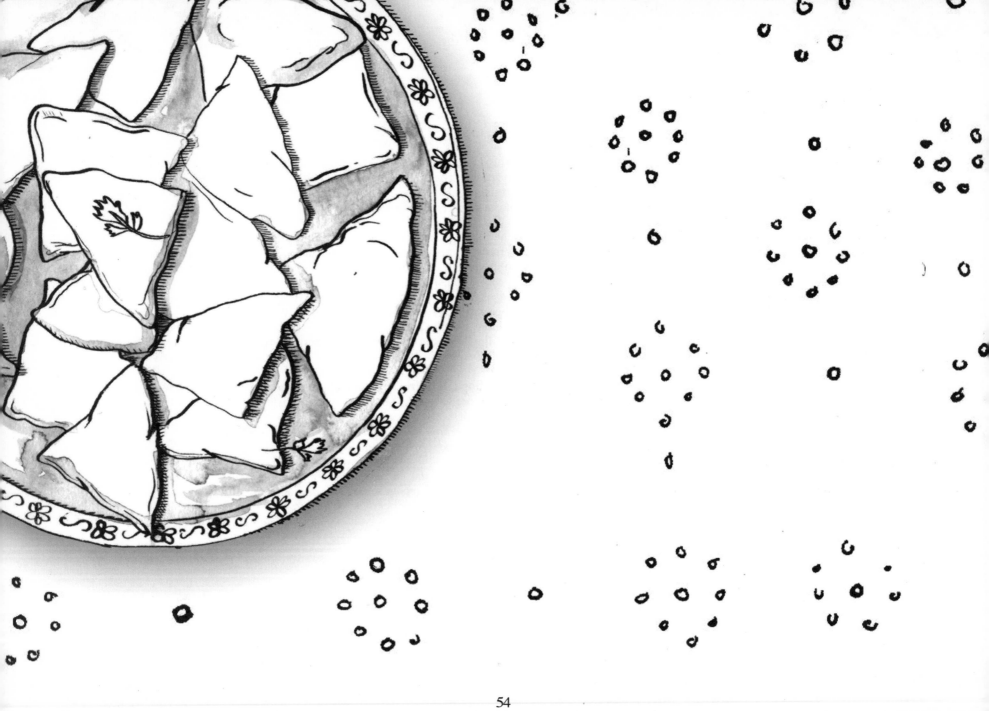

SAMOSA

Cooking time:
60 - 70 minutes

Pastry

1 cup plain flour
½ teaspoon salt
5 tablespoons oil
¼ cup water

Filling

6 medium potatoes
(boiled in skin, peeled and broken up into small pieces)
2 tablespoons peas (optional)
1 tablespoon coriander powder
½ teaspoon crushed chillies
¼ teaspoon turmeric powder
1 teaspoon salt
1 tablespoon pomegranate seeds
5 tablespoons oil
½ teaspoon cumin seeds
1 teaspoon asafoetida

OIL FOR FRYING

Pastry: Rub the oil into the flour till it turns into crumbly flakes. Mix in the salt. Add the water a bit at a time and gently knead into a springy dough. Leave sitting for half an hour.

Filling: Heat the oil in a frying pan. Add the cumin seeds. When browned, add asafoetida. As soon as it bubbles, add the potatoes and other spices. Mix gently and let it cook for 10 minutes on low heat, stirring the mixture from time to time. When the mixture is cold divide it into 10 to 12 portions.

Divide the pastry dough into 5 to 6 balls. Roll out each ball into a thin round puri. Cut the puri into 2 halves. Dip your index finger in water, wet the cut edge of the puri and shape the half into a cone. Press and seal the watered edge. Fill the cone with 1 portion of the potato mixture. Wet the open edge of the cone and seal the mixture in. Repeat the process till all the samosas are filled. Fry the samosas on both sides till golden in just above medium hot oil. Serve hot with sour mint chutney (pg 243) and sweet tamarind (pg 248).

This dish can be fried earlier and put under a hot grill for a few minutes before serving.

I always associate samosas with 2 things - breakfast and special people. In Baripada, when her son-in-laws visited her, my naniji always served samosas and rasgullas (a sweet made from paneer) bought from the local shop, all freshly made. It was customary for Grandma's generation to treat the son-in-laws like dignitaries. Finding quality samosas, made commercially, outside the sub-continent is not easy and although making them at home is a hard slog, it is certainly worth the effort as you get something just as you would like it.

BATATA WADDA

Cooking time:
30 - 40 minutes

Filling

8 medium size potatoes
(boiled in skin, peeled and broken into small pieces)
1-2 table spoon chopped green chilli
¼ cup green coriander leaves (chopped)
10 -12 curry leaves
handful small pieces of fresh coconut (optional)
1 teaspoon salt
1 teaspoon mustard seeds
4 tablespoons oil

Batter

1½ cup gram flour
½ teaspoon salt
½ teaspoon soda bicarbonate
¾ cup of water

OIL FOR FRYING

Heat the 4 tablespoons of oil in a good size wok or frying pan. Drop the mustard seeds in the oil and as soon as they pop, add the potatoes and all the other filling ingredients.

Leave cooking for at least 10 minutes on very low heat, stirring the mixture from time to time. Leave the potatoes to cool. When the mixture is cold divide it into 12 to 16 portions and roll each into a round shape.

Together with one tablespoon of oil and water, mix the batter ingredients to a thick soup consistency. Dip the potato balls into the batter and fry on both sides in the hot oil till golden. Serve hot with chutney of choice.

This dish can be fried earlier and put under a hot grill for few minutes before serving.

This is also called bonda and is a Mumbai speciality. Often two of these pressed inside a paav (another Mumbai special - a roll-size loaf of white bread), picked up on our way to school, served us as the most enjoyable lunch.

TIKKI 1

Cooking time:
30 - 35 minutes

10 medium size potatoes
(boiled in skin, peeled and mashed)
1 table spoon chopped green chilli
¼ cup chopped green coriander leaves
1 tea spoon salt

10 TABLESPOONS OIL
(for shallow frying)

Mix all the ingredients together well. Divide it into 12 to 16 portions and roll each into a round flat shape (tikki).

Coat each tikki on both sides with oil. Heat the remaining oil in a shallow frying pan and place in as many tikkis as possible. Lower the heat and let them gently turn brown and crispy on both sides. Serve hot with sour mint chutney (pg 243) and sweet tamarind (pg 248).

It is not recommended to reheat this dish.

No matter how many of these I make, there never seem to be enough for my family and friends.

TIKKI 2

Cooking time:
30 - 35 minutes

8 medium size potatoes
(boiled in skin, peeled and mashed)
1 tablespoon chopped green chilli
¼ cup chopped green coriander leaves
3 slices of dry white bread (crumbled into tiny pieces)
OR ½ cup bread crumbs
1 teaspoon salt

OIL FOR FRYING

Mix all the ingredients together well. Divide it into 12 to 16 portions and roll each into a round flat shape (tikki).

Heat the oil in a wok or frying pan and fry the tikkis till golden brown and crispy on both sides. Serve hot with sour mint chutney (pg 243) and sweet tamarind (pg 248).

(It is not recommended to reheat this dish.)

MUMBAI STYLE TIKKI (Ragdda Patis)

Cooking time:
60 minutes

Chick peas

1½ cup boiled chick peas (slightly mashed)
1 large onion (chopped into rough pieces)
½ teaspoon salt
1 teaspoon coriander seeds (crushed roughly)
½ teaspoon crushed chilli
4 tablespoons oil

Salad

1 medium red onion
3 inches of cucumber
2 leaves of crispy lettuce
(all thinly sliced)

Chick Peas: Fry the onions in hot oil till golden, add all other ingredients and cook gently for 10 minutes.

Serving Method: Place 2 hot tikkis * onto each plate with 1 ladle full of hot chick peas and some salad mix. Pour 1 tablespoon of sweet tamarind chutney on the peas. Serve hot with sour mint chutney (pg 243) and sweet tamarind (pg 248) on the side.

*see Tikki 1 recipe

This dish works better as a snack than as a starter.

We would start drooling just at the thought of eating this at a famous eatery in Mumbai. For me, ragdda-patis was always followed by faaluda (an elaborate ice-cream concoction) and after that I was in the seventh-food-heaven.

CORN WADDA

Cooking time:
30 minutes

1 cup fine corn flour
½ cup sour yoghurt
½ cup water
1 green chilli (finely chopped)
¼ cup green coriander leaves (chopped)
1 tablespoon ginger paste
1 tablespoon garlic paste
2 tablespoons sesame seeds
¾ teaspoon salt
½ teaspoon sugar

OIL FOR FRYING

Mix all the ingredients and add the water gently to make a thick batter. Using a spoon or hand, drop small dollops of the paste in the hot oil and fry on both sides till golden brown. Serve with a chutney of your choice.

A tea time treat courtesy of my Gujarati friend Shobha. Shobha has been part of my Sakhi (female friend) group for years. Bandi, my sister, and long time friend Prabha are the other members of this Sakhi group, which has often been called 'the mafia' by some of our family members. We as individuals have survived through the highs and lows of life with the other sakhis' support, love, care, sense of humour and, of course, food.

MUTHIA

Cooking time:
30 minutes

1 cup gram flour
¼ cup semolina
1 green chilli (chopped fine)
¼ cup green coriander (chopped fine)
OR dry oregano leaves
1 cup grated courgette
OR cabbage (red or green)
OR 1 medium leek stalk finely chopped
OR 1 cup chopped green fenugreek leaves
1 teaspoon salt
¼ teaspoon sugar
¼ cup oil

Baghaar

1 tablespoon oil
1 tablespoon of sesame seeds
1 teaspoon of mustard seeds
6-8 curry leaves

Mix all the ingredients together into a thick paste (if too soft, add more semolina).(Add water only if using leek or fenugreek). Drop bite size pieces into a well-oiled metal dish and steam cook for 15 to 20 minutes.

Baghaar: Heat the oil in a small pan and add the mustard seeds. As soon as they pop, add all other baghaar ingredients. Serve hot with coconut chutney 2 (pg 245).

This goes well with tea. But salty lassi is an equally good accompaniment.

CHILLAS (Pancakes)

Cooking time:
30 minutes

1½ cup gram flour
1 medium size onion (finely chopped)
¼ cup of green coriander leaves (chopped)
1 very finely chopped green chilli (optional)
1 tablespoon of oil
½ teaspoon of salt
½ cup of water

4 TABLESPOONS OF OIL
(for shallow frying)

Mix all ingredients plus 1 spoon of oil well together. The mixture should be of a thick soup consistency - therefore add more water if required (the mix should make around 6 chillas - but you can vary the size to your liking and get less or more).

Heat a frying pan and brush it with ½ spoon of oil and spread out a small ladle full of mix on the hot oil. leave it to cook till the top looks dry. Sprinkle ½ spoon of oil and turn it over to cook the other side. Both sides should be nicely browned. Repeat the process till all the chillas are done. Serve hot with tomato chutney (pg 246).

This can be made earlier and re-heated.

Savoury pancakes made with different flours make a good nutritional lunch/tea time snack for children and adults alike.

UTTHAPUM

Cooking time:
30 minutes

1½ cup of semolina
1 medium size onion (finely chopped)
1 small tomato (chopped fine)
¼ cup of green coriander leaves (chopped)
1 very finely chopped green chilli (optional)
¼ cup of grated coconut (optional)
¾ teaspoon of salt
¼ cup of sour yoghurt
¼ cup of water

4 TABLESPOONS OF OIL
(for shallow frying)

Mix all ingredients plus 1 spoon of oil well together. The mixture should be of a thick soup consistency, therefore add more water if required. The mix should make around 6 utthapums (you can vary the size to your liking).

Heat a frying pan and brush it with ½ spoon of oil and spread out a small ladle full of mix on the hot oil. Leave it to cook till the top looks dry. Sprinkle ½ spoon of oil and turn it over to cook the other side. Both sides should be nicely browned. Repeat the process till all the utthapums are done. Serve hot with coconut chutney 3 (pg 245).

Does not taste so good when re-heated.

Dals

All dals and beans, besides being delicious, are rich in high quality proteins. But some have these proteins in higher proportions, such as urad dal and whole urad. Dal and beans are also high in roughage. They are one of the main elements of a balanced vegetarian diet. They are also regularly used for beauty treatments across India. When cooking, most dals take 20 to 30 minutes to soften (depending on the water – hard or soft). But the fastest cooking dal is masoor dal – it takes around 10 minutes to go mushy. Black-eyed beans take about twenty minutes but the rest of the beans take much longer to cook.

Beans and dals come in many varieties. Most Indian vegetarian households cook a different dal or bean each day, accompanied by suitable vegetables and other sundries. Most dals are in fact beans split and de-husked, thereby losing some of the roughage but becoming lighter to digest. For this reason, beans are generally considered party food while dals are part of a daily diet.

Tips:

- Most beans, except black-eyed beans, can take as much as 25 to 30 minutes to cook, therefore it is advisable to use a pressure cooker.

- Always soak the beans for 3 to 4 hours before boiling. This cuts the cooking time and saves energy.

- Soak the dal for at least an hour prior to cooking.

- Do not throw away the water that the dal or beans have been soaked in. Some nutrients are lost in doing so. Use the same water to boil the dal/beans.

- When you put dal or beans to boil, normally at the point of boiling a certain amount of froth will accumulate at the top. Skim this off. This helps reduce the gaseousness of the dal or bean. Normally, ginger is added to most beans and some dals to counter act their gas producing property.

The variety of dals and beans one can use is vast. However, the main type of dals and beans I have used for recipes in this book are:

CHANA (Chick-peas) come in two types – white, slightly larger peas generally referred to as Kabuli Chana, and brown or green skinned, smaller peas generally referred to as 'Kala (black) Chana'. It is the smaller peas that are split and de-husked to give us chana dal (split-pea lentil). Chana dal is very versatile in that it can be used just for making dals or making other savoury or sweet dishes with its flour. The dal is shiny yellow in colour and when ground produces besen (gram flour) which is then used for making dishes such as kaddhi, pakoras or panjeeri.

LOBHIYA (Black-eyed beans) so called because of the black dots on one side, are small, cream coloured beans, easy to boil and can be prepared on their own or with a variety of vegetables. They are also good for making light, crispy fritters.

MASOOR (Brown/Red lentils) – brown masoor is the whole dal with the skin on. Split and de-skinned they can be anything from orange to red in colour but are commonly known as red lentils. This colour changes to creamy-yellow when cooked. Both take a short time to cook and can be dished out in many different ways.

MOONG is perhaps the smallest bean. Green in colour, when skinned and split produces the pale yellow moong dal. Both cook in a reasonable time and are the lightest of all the dals and beans to digest. In fact, a person recuperating from illness is fed with a soupy version of this dal as it is high in nourishment and yet easy to digest. It can also be used for making the famous dessert, Moong Halva.

RAJMA (Red kidney beans) so named because of their shape and colour, when cooked, give a rich look to a meal. Their cooking time is long but their taste makes it worthwhile.

TOOR/ARHAR is rarely used as a whole bean. The dal is light yellow in colour and is commonly used throughout India. It is equally delicious plain with some lemon juice as cooked in Uttar Pradesh region or as highly spiced Sambhar from South India.

URAD has in common the same shape and size as moong. But, its skin is matt black, takes longer to cook and is much heavier to digest. Mixed in the whole urad are small extremely hard beans, black but slightly shinier and smaller than urad. These need to be weeded out prior to cooking or they play havoc with your teeth and fillings. However, the effort is worth it as it is a very tasty dal. The split de-skinned urad provides the cream colour urad dal. When cooked, urad beans and dal have a creamy texture. Its flour, mixed in with rice flour, is used for South Indian dishes such as dosas and idlies.

All cooked dals and beans can be frozen. They retain their texture and taste well.

The preparation time for dals and beans may seem quite long, but don't be put off by this as most of this time is for boiling and softening the dal/beans. The time required for spicing and baghaar is the small part of it.

Baddi

Baddi is dehydrated lentil dumpling used as and when required. Basically the 'fiendishly clever' Indians found another way of preserving lentils long term by using all of nature's resources. Lentils are soaked and ground to a rough thick paste. Salt, chilli and herbs are added according to taste and dumplings dropped on a clean cloth and left to dry in the hot Indian sun. Once absolutely dried, they are stored in air-tight jars and used whenever needed. Mainly two types of baddis are commercially available - large spicy ones with whole black pepper in them (also called Punjabi baddi as they are from that region) and small ones (also called mangaudi) with herbs. Both are easily available in South Asian grocery stores. A third variety is fresh baddi made with moong or masoor dal. Lentils are soaked and ground to a fine thick paste. Salt, chilli and herbs added according to taste, the dumplings are dropped into hot oil, fried till crispy brown and then used for a dish.

LARGE BADDI

Cooking time:
20 minutes

2 large baddis (broken into 6 pieces)
1 large potato
(peeled and chopped into 8 pieces)
1 large tomato (chopped into 8 pieces)
1 teaspoon of coriander powder
¼ teaspoon of crushed chillies
¼ teaspoon of turmeric
1 teaspoon of salt
2 cups of water

Baghaar

4 tablespoons of oil
OR 2 tablespoons of ghee
½ teaspoon of cumin seeds
½ teaspoon of asafoetida

Heat oil / ghee in a pot, add the baddi pieces and roast on a gentle heat until browned on all sides. Take the baddi pieces out and add cumin seeds and asafoetida to the same oil/ghee. When browned add potatoes and all other ingredients (except tomatoes).

Stir well and cook on low heat for 5 minutes and add baddis and tomatoes. Stir for 2 to 3 minutes, add water and bring to boil. Simmer on low heat till baddi and potatoes are cooked (the dish should have a thick gravy).

The dish can also be cooked with aubergine or marrow:
Replace the potato with aubergine or marrow (approx ¼ kg) chopped into medium size pieces.

Best served with parathas or rotis.

Eating these large baddis, wedged with whole black peppers and coriander seeds, always takes me back to when I travelled with my naniji, aunt and uncle to Banares, Allahabad, Delhi, Dehradun, etc. While the grown-ups focused on finding a bride for my uncle, I absorbed all the flavours, tastes and smells of the variety of food we were being treated to. The baddi in rich gravy would be served with parathas that were ever so crispy on the outside and had soft layers within. One would scoop the baddi and gravy with a piece of paratha and experience a burst of tastes and textures in the mouth – hot and spicy, crisp and creamy, all blended together to form a perfect morsel.

SMALL BADDI

Cooking time:
20 minutes

1 cup of small baddis
2 large tomatoes
(chopped into small pieces)
OR 200g tinned
1 teaspoon of coriander powder
¼ teaspoon of crushed chillies
¼ teaspoon of turmeric
1 teaspoon of salt
1½ cups of water
¼ cup of green coriander leaves (chopped)

Baghaar

2 tablespoons of butter / ghee
½ teaspoon of cumin seeds
½ teaspoon of asafoetida

Heat butter/ghee in a pot, add the baddi and roast on gentle heat till browned on all sides. Add cumin seeds and asafoetida. When browned add tomatoes and all other ingredients. Stir well and cook on low heat for 5 minutes. Add water and bring to boil.

Simmer on low heat till baddis are cooked. (The dish should have a thin gravy). Sprinkle green coriander leaves over the dish before serving.

Almost every household in small towns and villages would have fresh baddis drying on their terraces or yard in the scorching summer sun and children like me were put on duty to guard them against birds – and in Banares, monkeys!

FRESH BADDI

Cooking time:
35 minutes

Baddi

**1 cup of moong
OR masoor dal
(soaked for at least 2 hours)
1 tablespoon of yoghurt**

OIL FOR FRYING

Gravy

**2 large tomatoes
(chopped into small pieces)
OR 200g tin
1 teaspoon coriander powder
½ teaspoon crushed chillies
¼ teaspoon of turmeric
¾ teaspoon of salt
1½ cup of water
¼ cup green coriander leaves (chopped)**

Baghaar

**2 tablespoons of butter / ghee
½ teaspoon of cumin seeds
½ teaspoon of asafoetida**

Baddi: Drain the water from the dal and paste it in a grinder. Mix in ¼ teaspoon of salt and yoghurt. Whisk the mixture well for 2 to 3 minutes.

Heat the oil in a wok and using fingers, carefully drop in 16 to 20 rounded dollops of dal paste (baddis). When the baddis are well browned, remove from the oil and put them aside.

Gravy: Heat butter / ghee in pot and add cumin seeds and asafoetida. When browned add the tomatoes and all other ingredients. Stir well and cook on a low heat for 5 minutes.

Add water and bring to boil. Add the baddis. Simmer on a low heat for 4 to 5 minutes (This dish should have a thin gravy)

Before serving, sprinkle the coriander.

My aunt used to make this the best. I used to watch her grind the dal to a paste on a stone slab (sil-batta) and then whip the paste with hand until it was aerated and fluffy: the end result was melt-in-your-mouth dumplings floating in subtly spiced gravy.

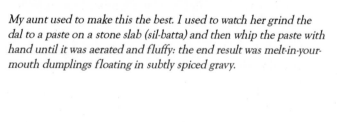

BLACK EYED BEANS (with tomatoes)

Cooking time:
35 - 40 minutes

1 cup of black eyed beans
1 tablespoon of coriander powder
½ teaspoon of turmeric
¼ teaspoon of chilli powder
1 teaspoon of salt
1 large tomato
(chopped into 6 - 8 pieces)
¼ cup of green coriander leaves (chopped)

Baghaar

2 tablespoons of ghee / butter
½ teaspoon of cumin seeds
1 large onion (finely chopped)
1 tablespoon of ginger
(finely chopped)
1 tablespoon of garlic
(finely chopped)

Wash and soak the beans in 4 cups of water for at least 2 hours. Place in a pan, heat and bring it to boil and remove the froth that gathers at the top. Then, lower the heat and simmer for 15 to 20 minutes until soft (A pressure cooker can boil them in about 3 to 5 minutes).

Add the salt and simmer for 2 to 3 minutes and take it off the heat. Make sure that the liquid in the pan does not evaporate. Add more water if necessary.

Heat ghee / butter in a pan, add cumin seeds and as soon as these brown, add onions. Fry until golden, add ginger, garlic, coriander, turmeric and chilli powder. Stir for a few seconds.

Add the tomatoes, cook for 4 to 5 minutes and mix in the cooked beans with the liquid and let the mixture simmer for 5 to 7 minutes. Sprinkle green coriander and serve.

This dish can be made without onion and garlic – just like in my grandmother's home!

I did not get to eat these beans, cooked in onion and garlic, until we moved to Mumbai in the 1950s and had a meal in a Punjabi restaurant. I just loved the taste of this tangy, spicy blend with rotis.

BLACK EYED BEANS WITH BHINDI (Okra)

Cooking time:
45 minutes

¾ cup of black eyed beans
16 - 20 bhindi (tops and tails snipped)
2 large tomatoes (chopped into 8 - 10 pieces)
1 medium sized potato (cut into 8 piece)
1 tablespoon of coriander powder
½ teaspoon of turmeric
¼ teaspoon of chilli powder
1 teaspoons of salt
¼ cup of green coriander leaves (chopped)

OIL FOR FRYING

Baghaar

2 tablespoons of ghee / butter
½ teaspoons of cumin seeds
1 large onion (finely chopped)
1 tablespoon of ginger (finely chopped)
1 tablespoon of garlic (finely chopped)

Wash and soak the beans in 4 cups of water for at least 2 hours. Place in a pan, heat and bring it to boil and remove the froth that gathers at the top. Lower the heat and simmer for 15 to 20 minutes until soft (A pressure cooker can boil them in about 3 to 5 minutes).

While the beans are boiling, deep fry the potatoes in medium hot oil. Next, fry the bhindi in very hot oil and put them aside.

Add salt to the beans and simmer for 2 to 3 minutes and take it off the heat. Make sure that the liquid in the pan does not evaporate. Add more water if necessary.

Heat the ghee / butter in a pan, add the cumin seeds and as soon as these brown add the onion. Fry until golden, add the ginger, garlic, coriander, turmeric and chilli powder and stir for few seconds. Add tomatoes, cook for 4 to 5 minutes and mix in the cooked beans with its liquid. Add the potatoes and let the mixture simmer for 5 to 7 minutes. Gently mix in the bhindi, cook for another minute. Sprinkle green coriander and serve.

Our Sindhi neighbour used to bring a bowlful of this dish for us every time she cooked it, for she knew how much we enjoyed it. Needless to say, my mother would always send over dishes which the neighbour and her family liked.

BLACK EYED BEANS WITH MUSHROOMS

Cooking time:
35 minutes

¾ cup of black eyed beans
200g of mushrooms
(chopped into medium sized pieces)
1 tablespoon of coriander powder
¼ teaspoon of turmeric
¼ teaspoon of chilli powder
½ teaspoon of garam masala
½ teaspoon of fennel powder
1 teaspoon of salt
¼ cup of green coriander leaves (chopped)

Baghaar

2 tablespoons of ghee / butter
½ teaspoon of cumin seeds
1 large onion (finely chopped)
1 tablespoon of garlic (finely chopped)

Wash and soak the beans in 4 cups of water for at least 2 hours, place in a pan, heat and bring it to the boil and remove the froth that gathers at the top. Lower the heat and simmer for 15 to 20 minutes until soft.
(A pressure cooker can boil them in about 3 to 5 minutes)

Add salt and simmer for 2 to 3 minutes and take it off the heat. Make sure that the liquid in the pan does not evaporate. Add more water if necessary.

Heat the ghee / butter in a pan, add the cumin seeds and as soon as these brown add the onion. Fry until golden, add garlic, coriander, turmeric, garam masala, fennel and chilli powder and stir for a few seconds.

Add the mushrooms, cook for 2 to 3 minutes and mix in the cooked beans with liquid and let the mixture simmer for 5 to 7 minutes. Sprinkle with green coriander and serve.

I had this at a party in London, given by my best friend Prabha. Everyone should have a friend like Prabha. No matter how bad the situation is, no matter where either of us is in the world, we talk and manage to have a laugh and a joke and dissipate some of the anxiety and stress. But, when we are together, Priya, my daughter observes that, she has not come across anyone talk about food as much as Prabha, myself and other sakhis do - particularly as we are so keen to lose weight!

CHANA DAL (Plain)

Cooking time:
25 minutes

1 cup of chana dal
(washed and soaked in 5 cups of water)
½ teaspoon of coriander powder
¼ teaspoon of turmeric
¼ teaspoon of chilli powder
1 teaspoon of salt
4 - 5 tablespoons of lemon juice
1 tablespoon of ginger - finely chopped
(optional)

Baghaar

1 tablespoon of ghee or butter
½ teaspoon of cumin seeds
½ teaspoon of asafoetida

Bring the dal to boil and remove the froth that gathers at the top. Add coriander, turmeric, chillies and ginger (if used) and cover the pot with lid. Lower heat and simmer for 10 to 15 minutes (until soft).

Add salt and lemon juice. Mix well (the consistency should be like a thick soup therefore add water if necessary). Simmer for 2 to 3 minutes and take it off the heat.

Heat ghee / butter in a small pan or bowl. Add cumin seeds and asafoetida, as soon as these brown turn the heat off. Spread the mixture evenly on top of the cooked dal, gently stir and serve.

In North India, and therefore in my grandmother's home, all dals were served with extra ghee / butter on top, thus adding further fragrance and taste to the dal. I being an unreserved dairy product lover (and it shows) as a child, was never satisfied with the amount of ghee poured on my dal and used to beg my naniji for more and again for more and more. It's not for nothing that Prabha, my sakhi, calls me 'the dairy queen'.

CHANA DAL (with Onions)

Cooking time:
30 minutes

1 cup of chana dal
(washed and soaked in 5 cups of water)
½ teaspoon of coriander powder
¼ teaspoon of turmeric
¼ teaspoon of crushed chilli
1 teaspoon of salt
1 tablespoon of ginger - finely chopped (optional)

Baghaar

2 tablespoons of ghee or butter
½ teaspoon of cumin seeds
1 large onion (chopped thin lenghtwise)
2 whole red chillies

Bring the dal to boil and remove the froth that gathers at the top. Add coriander, turmeric, chillies and ginger (if used) and cover the pot with lid. Lower heat and simmer for 10 to 15 minutes (until soft).

Add salt and mix well (the consistency should be like a thick soup, therefore add water if necessary). Simmer for 2 to 3 minutes and take it off the heat.

Heat ghee / butter in a small pan and add cumin seeds. As soon as these brown, add onions and fry until golden. Add the whole chillies and turn the heat off. Spread the mixture evenly on top of the cooked dal, gently stir and serve.

The fried onion and whole chillies add tempting colour and flavour to this dish making it that bit extra special. My partner, Gordon, can live on dals of any kind. This is one of his favourites.

CHANA DAL (Sweet and Sour)

Cooking time:
30 minutes

1 cup of chana dal
(washed and soaked in 5 cups of water)
1 teaspoon of coriander powder
¼ teaspoon of turmeric
¼ teaspoon of crushed chilli
1¼ teaspoons of salt
1-2 tablespoons of tamarind pulp
OR 4 - 5 tablespoons of lemon juice
2 - 3 teaspoons of sugar
¼ cup green coriander leaves (chopped)

Baghaar

1 tablespoon of ghee or butter
½ teaspoon of cumin seeds
1 tablespoon of ginger (finely chopped)
1 tablespoon of garlic (finely chopped)

Bring the dal to boil and remove the froth that gathers at the top. Add coriander, turmeric and chillies and cover the pot with lid. Lower heat and simmer for 10 to 15 minutes (until soft and mushy).

Add salt, sugar and tamarind or lemon juice and mix well (the consistency should be in between thick and thin soup, therefore, add water if necessary). Simmer for 2 to 3 minutes and take it off the heat.

Heat the ghee / butter in a small pan and add cumin seeds. As soon as these brown, add ginger and garlic and fry until golden. Turn the heat off. Spread the mixture evenly on top of the cooked dal, gently stir and serve.

I find this dal irresistible with thin rotis. But it's equally appealing with rice. Not bad either on its own as a soup.

CHANA DAL WITH SPINACH

Cooking time:
40 minutes

½ cup of chana dal
(washed and soaked in 1 ½ cups of water)
1 teaspoon of coriander powder
½ teaspoon of turmeric
¼ teaspoon of chilli powder
1 teaspoon of salt
¼ kg of spinach (finely chopped)
1 bunch of fresh dill finely chopped (optional)
1 tablespoon of ginger (finely crushed)
1 tablespoon of garlic (finely crushed)

Baghaar

2 tablespoons of ghee or butter
½ teaspoon of cumin seeds
1 large onion (finely chopped)
2 medium tomatoes (chopped into 16 pieces)

Bring the dal to boil and remove the froth that gathers at the top. Add coriander, turmeric, chillies, garlic and ginger and cover the pot with lid. Lower heat and simmer for 10 to 15 minutes (until soft). Add spinach and dill (if used) and cook until the mixture is mushy.

Add salt and mix with a heavy spoon or blender almost to a puree (the consistency should be like a thick soup, therefore add water if necessary). Simmer for 2 to 3 minutes and take it off the heat.

Heat ghee / butter in a small pan and add cumin seeds, as soon as these brown add onions and fry until golden. Stir in the tomatoes and mix the lot well into the dal. Cook the mixture for 4 to 5 minutes and serve.

This is another recipe that I have happily replicated,
courtesy of our Sindhi neighbours in Mumbai.

CHANA DAL WITH COURGETTE or Marrow or Lauki

Cooking time:
40 minutes

½ cup of chana dal
(washed and soaked in 2 cups of water)
¼ kg of courgette or marrow or lauki
(chopped into 1 inch cube)
1 teaspoon of coriander powder
¼ teaspoon of turmeric
¼ teaspoon of crushed chilli
½ teaspoon of garam masala
1 teaspoon of salt
¼ cup of green coriander leaves (chopped)

Baghaar

2 tablespoons of ghee or butter
½ teaspoon of cumin seeds
1 large onion (finely chopped)
1 tablespoon ginger (finely chopped)
1 tablespoon garlic (finely chopped)

Heat ghee / butter in a pan, add cumin seeds and as soon as these brown, add onions and fry until golden brown. Add garlic and ginger and lower heat to minimum and mix in all the dry spices (except salt). Stir for a few seconds.

Add the dal and water, bring to boil and cook for 5 to 7 minutes on a gentle heat. Add the marrow (or the vegetable of choice), salt and cook until the dal and the marrow are tender (approximately 10 to 12 minutes). Make sure that it has a bit of gravy. Sprinkle with coriander and serve.

This recipe can be cooked without onion and garlic except that you add ½ teaspoon of asafoetida after browning the cumin seeds.

I find this blending of vegetable and dal not only tasty but also providing a combination of nutrients. This means I can get away with cooking one dish and serve it with a salad and yoghurt. This dish goes best with parathas but is good with rice as well.

CHANA DAL WITH CAULIFLOWER AND COCONUT

Cooking time:
30 minutes

½ cup of chana dal
(washed and soaked in 1 ½ cups of water)
1 small (approx. ¼ kg) cauliflower
(chopped medium size pieces)
1 teaspoon of coriander powder
¼ teaspoon of chilli powder
1 teaspoon of salt
¼ cup of green coriander leaves (chopped)

Baghaar

2 tablespoons of oil
½ teaspoon of mustard seeds
1 large onion (finely chopped)
½ cup of fresh or dry coconut (desiccated)
OR 3 tablespoons coconut cream
1 tablespoon of garlic (finely chopped)
8 -10 curry leaves

Heat oil in a pan and add mustard seeds, as soon as these pop add the onions and fry until translucent and mix in the coconut.

Add garlic, curry leaves and all dry spices (except salt). Stir for a few seconds, add the dal, cover with water, bring to boil and cook for 5 to 6 minutes on a gentle heat.

Add the cauliflower and salt and cook until the dal and cauliflower are tender (approximately 10 minutes).

Sprinkle with fresh coriander and serve.

My Irani school friend, Katie, not only initiated me to alcohol at the age of 19 but also introduced me to Irani /Parsi dishes which are so very different from North Indian fare – a culmination of Persian (it is Persia that Parsi/ Irani people migrated from), and West Coast Indian cuisine. I loved both food and alcohol; and still do. But it's the food I love best.

KALA CHANA (Plain)

Cooking time:
45 minutes

1 cup of whole chana (black)
(washed and soaked in 4 cups of water)
1 teaspoon of coriander powder
¼ teaspoon of turmeric
¼ teaspoon of crushed chilli
1 teaspoon of salt
1 tablespoon of ginger (finely chopped)
3 - 4 tablespoons of lemon juice
¼ cup of green coriander leaves (chopped)

Baghaar

1 tablespoon of ghee
OR 2 tablespoons of oil
½ teaspoon of cumin seeds
½ teaspoon of asafoetida

Bring to boil the chana with coriander, turmeric and chillies and ginger. Lower the heat and simmer for 20 to 25 minutes (until soft). (A pressure cooker can boil them in 10 minutes)

Add salt (there should be some liquid covering the chana, therefore add water if necessary) and simmer for 2 to 3 minutes and take it off the heat.

Heat ghee / oil in a small pan. Add cumin seeds and asofoetida and as soon these brown, mix in the chana and lemon juice then cook for a few minutes. Sprinkle with coriander before serving.

I like this chana best with puris. But it makes a heavy meal so it is best served with a light salad and yoghurt. I also like it because kala chana never goes mushy, unless you mush it - I do enjoy food that one can chew on.

KALA CHANA (Dry)

Cooking time:
40 minutes

1 cup of whole chana
(washed and soaked in 3 cups of water)
½ teaspoon of coriander powder
¼ teaspoon of turmeric
¼ teaspoon of chilli powder
¾ teaspoon of salt

Baghaar

2 tablespoons of oil
½ teaspoon of cumin seeds
½ teaspoon of asafoetida
1 green chilli cut lengthways into 4

Bring chana to boil, with coriander, turmeric and chillies. Lower heat and simmer for 20 to 25 minutes (until soft). (A pressure cooker can boil them in about 7 minutes)

Add salt and simmer until all liquid dries out. Heat oil in a pan, add cumin seeds and asafoetida, and as soon these brown, add the chana, mix well and cook for a few minutes. Serve decorated with green chilli.

This dish always reminds me of the Hindu festival in which, once a year, young girls are given the status of Devi (goddess), their feet washed, a prayer performed and then they are treated to a special meal of dry chana, puris and semolina halva. The best part for most of us was getting some money at the end of this ritual.

KALA CHANA WITH POTATOES (Chana Bateta)

Cooking time:
55 minutes

1 cup of black chana
(washed and soaked in 5 cups of water)
1 medium potato (chopped into 8 - 10 pieces)
1 teaspoon of coriander powder
½ teaspoon of turmeric
¼ teaspoon of chilli powder
1¼ teaspoons of salt
½ teaspoon of sugar
¼ cup of green coriander leaves (chopped)

Baghaar

6 tablespoons of oil
½ teaspoon of mustard seeds
1 large onions (finely chopped)
1 tablespoon of ginger (finely chopped)
1 tablespoon of garlic (finely chopped)
8 - 10 curry leaves

Bring chana to boil with coriander, turmeric and chillies. Lower heat and simmer for 20 to 25 minutes (until soft). (A pressure cooker can boil them in about 7 minutes). Add salt, simmer for 2 to 3 minutes (there should be some liquid covering the chana therefore add water if necessary) and take it off the heat.

Heat the oil in a pan. Add mustard seeds and as soon as these brown, add onions. Fry until golden, add ginger, garlic, curry leaves and potatoes and stir for 1 to 2 minutes. Add the cooked chana with liquid and let the mixture simmer until the potatoes are cooked. Sprinkle green coriander and serve.

This dish can be made without the potato.

This can also be made in a sweet and sour style:
add 1 to 2 tablespoons of fresh tamarind paste and 1 to 2 teaspoons of sugar after the potato is cooked. Plus add about ¼ teaspoon of extra salt.

This is a Gujarati style dish, courtesy of my Gujarati friends and family in London. It is delicious with puris or rice.

KABULI CHANA (Chick Peas) - (Dry)

Cooking time:
40 minutes

1 cup chick peas (washed and soaked in 3 cups of water)
OR ready cooked 800g tin
1 teaspoon of coriander powder
¼ teaspoon of turmeric
¼ teaspoon of crushed chilli
1 teaspoon of salt (less for tinned chana)
¾ tablespoon of garam masala
1 tablespoon of fresh ginger paste
1 tablespoon of amchoor
OR 2 - 3 tablespoons lemon juice
¼ cup green coriander leaves (chopped)

Baghaar

6 tablespoons of oil
½ teaspoon of cumin seeds
½ teaspoon of asafoetida

Bring chick peas to the boil with coriander, turmeric and chillies. Lower heat and simmer for 25 to 35 minutes (until soft, but not mushy). (A pressure cooker can boil them in about 7 minutes). Add salt, simmer until all liquid dries out and take it off the heat. Alternatively if you are using tinned chick peas, drain most of the liquid from the can, add slightly less salt, ready for next stage.

Heat the oil in a pan. Add cumin seeds and asafoetida. As soon as these brown, add the chick peas, garam masala, ginger and amchoor (or lemon). Fry on gentle heat for 5 to 6 minutes. Sprinkle green coriander and serve.

To give this dish a distinct flavour and colour replace the amchoor / lemon juice with 2 to 3 tablespoons of smooth pomegranate paste.

For a variation to this recipe, it can be served with gravy by leaving some liquid in the chana when simmering rather than letting all the liquid dry out.

Although of the same family as the whole black chana, this one has a silkier texture and smoother taste. Yet it is equally heavy on the stomach. All the same, its sharp, sour taste is a nice contrast with puris.

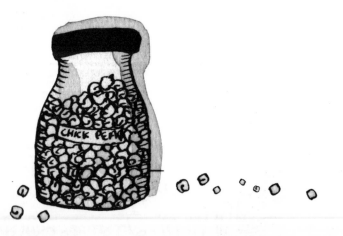

CHOLLE

Cooking time:
55 - 60 minutes

**1 cup of chickpeas
(washed and soaked in 5 cups of water)
OR 800g tinned
1½ teaspoons of coriander powder
1½ teaspoons of garam masala
½ teaspoon of turmeric
¼ teaspoon of crushed chilli
1½ teaspoons of salt
1 tablespoon of amchoor
OR 2 - 3 teaspoons of lemon juice
¼ cup of green coriander leaves (chopped)**

Baghaar

**8 tablespoons of oil
½ teaspoon of cumin seeds
1 large onion (finely chopped)
1 tablespoon of ginger (finely crushed)
1 tablespoon of garlic (finely crushed)
2 bay leaves
2 black cardamoms
2 small pieces of cinnamon sticks
2 - 3 whole green chillies**

Bring chana to boil. Lower heat and simmer for 25 to 35 minutes (until soft). (A pressure cooker can boil them in about 7 minutes). Add salt and simmer for 2 to 3 minutes (there should be some liquid i.e. enough covering the chana; therefore add water if necessary) and take it off the heat. Alternatively if you are using tinned chick peas, add about 1 teaspoon salt so it is ready for the next stage.

Heat the oil in a pan, add cumin seeds and as soon as these brown, add onions. Fry until golden, add ginger, garlic, cardamom and cinnamon and, stir for a few seconds. Add coriander, tumeric, garam masala and crushed chilli. Mix for a few seconds and add in the cooked chana with the liquid and let the mixture simmer for 10 to 15 minutes.

Add amchoor or lemon and simmer for 5 minutes. Sprinkle with green coriander and serve.

Near our house in Mumbai was a Punjabi market full of restaurants and dhabbas (traditional eateries). It was famous throughout the city for its fish dishes. But as a vegetarian family we never tasted the famous fare so I cannot vouch for its excellence, however what I can swear by is the Cholle-Bhature (Chana with plain flour puris) they served. On Sunday mornings, the boys (my younger brothers) would be sent out to get our brunch while two of the three sisters and dad sat and read the Sunday papers and my mum and one of the girls prepared the sweet, strong chai. This chai, along with green chillies, pickle and onion salad, was a perfect accompaniment for the pungent, zesty cholle and totally fluffed up, crispy bhature which we consumed with much chitter-chatter – every morsel an absolute delight.

KABULI CHANA (with Tomatoes)

Cooking time:
45 minutes

1 cup chick peas (washed and soaked in 4 cups of water)
OR 800g tin
2 large tomatoes (chopped into 16 pieces)
1½ teaspoons of coriander powder
¼ teaspoon of turmeric
¼ teaspoon of crushed chilli
1¼ teaspoons of salt
2 - 3 tablespoons of lemon juice
¼ cup of green coriander leaves (finely chopped)

Baghaar

2 tablespoons of ghee / butter
½ teaspoon of cumin seeds
1 large onions (finely chopped)
1 tablespoon of ginger (finely chopped)
1 tablespoon of garlic (finely chopped)

Bring the chick peas to boil. Lower heat and simmer for 25 to 35 minutes (until soft). (A pressure cooker can boil them in about 7 minutes)

Add the salt and simmer for 2 to 3 minutes (there should be some liquid covering the chana, therefore add water if necessary) and take it off the heat. Alternatively, if you are using tinned chick peas, add about 1 teaspoon salt so it is ready for the next stage.

Heat ghee / butter in a pan, add cumin seeds and as soon as these brown, add onions. Fry until golden, add ginger, garlic and stir for a few seconds. Add coriander, turmeric and chilli powder. Stir for 2 to 3 seconds, add tomatoes and cook for 4 to 5 minutes.

Add lemon juice and mix in the cooked chana with liquid and let the mixture simmer for a further 5 to 7 minutes (the chana should be floating in liquid, therefore add a bit of water if necessary). Sprinkle green coriander and serve.

This dish is one of my creations which I utterly love with rice.
Its tangy gravy, with the slight sweetness of tomato is a very
delicious concoction indeed.

KADDHI (Punjabi)

Cooking time:
50 minutes

Pakoras
¼ cup of gram flour
1 medium onion (chopped lengthways)
¼ cup of water
1 green chilli (chopped fine)
¼ cup green coriander leaves (chopped)
1 tablespoon of lemon juice
under ½ teaspoon of salt

OIL FOR FRYING

Kaddhi (sauce)
¼ cup of gram flour
2 cups of sour yoghurt
3 cups of water
½ teaspoon of coriander powder
¼ teaspoon of crushed chillies
¼ teaspoon of turmeric
1 teaspoon of salt
1 teaspoon of sugar

Baghaar
1 tablespoon of butter/ghee
½ teaspoon of cumin seeds
½ teaspoon of fenugreek seeds
½ teaspoon of asafoetida

Second Baghaar
2 tablespoons of butter/ghee
2 tablespoons of garlic optional (chopped fine)
½ teaspoon of paprika or chilli powder
2 dried whole red chillies

> Although not strictly a dal, I have put kaddhi in this section for two reasons: one, because its main ingredient is gram flour, and two, in any meal with kaddhi there is no need for dal or beans.

Pakoras

Mix all the ingredients together. Beat the mixture well for 2 to 3 minutes. Heat the oil in a wok and, using fingers, drop in rounded dollops of the mix into the hot oil (8 to 10 pakoras). When the pakoras are well browned, remove from the oil and put them aside.

Kaddhi

Mix the gram flour, water and spices making sure there are no lumps left in the mixture. Heat 1 spoon of ghee/butter in a pot, add cumin, fenugreek seeds and, when browned, add asafoetida. Stir in the liquid. Leaving it on high flame, keep stirring the mixture until it comes to boil (ensuring no lumps form). Simmer on a low heat for 10 minutes.

Beat the yoghurt and add to the liquid. Let it simmer on a low heat for another 15 to 20 minutes. (Consistency of the liquid should be as of a thick soup. Therefore, add water if needed.) Add the pakoras and cook for 2 to 3 minutes.

Second Baghaar:

Heat two spoons of ghee, add the whole chillies and garlic. When browned, add paprika, pour the mix on Kaddhi and serve.

My mother would kill me if I didn't include this dish – her most favourite food. Once she heard that I was writing a cook-book she started making regular, long calls from New Zealand, where she now lives, instructing me on various recipes. There was a time when the family used to quail at the mere mention of kaddhi as Maa used to make it so often. But now I wish she was here because, it has to be said, she made the best kadhhi you would taste. Her dad used to say that if Manorama has made the kaddhi then it will be perfect. She would serve this with crispy potatoes and sweet and sour pumpkin. I have followed her recipe in spirit, but, being partial to onion and garlic, I have jazzed up the pakoras somewhat with onions and added the second baghaar with garlic (this I picked up from my Pathan friend in school). So this is especially for you, Maa. Most Punjabis consider rice as the natural accompaniment for kaddhi but me being me, I love it with rotis.

KADDHI (Gujarati)

Cooking time:
60 minutes

1 tablespoon of gram flour
2 cups of sour yoghurt
4 cups of water
a good pinch of turmeric
1 teaspoon of salt
3 - 4 teaspoons of sugar
¼ cup green coriander leaves (chopped)
1 teaspoon of garlic paste (optional)
1 teaspoon of ginger (paste)
2 fresh green or dried whole red chillies
6 - 8 curry leaves

Baghaar

1 tablespoon of butter/ghee
½ teaspoon of cumin seeds
½ teaspoon of fenugreek seeds
½ teaspoon of mustard seeds
½ teaspoon of asafoetida

Mix the gram flour, turmeric, ginger, garlic, salt, sugar, yoghurt and water making sure there are no lumps left in the mixture.

Heat ghee/butter in a good size pot and add cumin, fenugreek, mustard seeds, red chillies (if using those). When browned, add asafoetida and curry leaves. Add the liquid. Leaving it on a high flame, keep stirring the mixture until it comes to the boil (ensuring no lumps form). Cook on a very low heat for 40-45 minutes. (Consistency should be like a thin soup, therefore add water if necessary)

Before serving, add the coriander and green chillies - split lengthways. (if using those)

This blend, with its subtle flavour of ginger, curry leaves and other condiments is a real treat with rice or roti. Above and beyond being tasty, this kaddhi is a real comfort in winter or when one is suffering from a sore throat, cough and/or cold. The thin, sour and sweet liquid sooths the itchy-scratchy throat just so and helps clear up the blocked up nose. My father-in-law used to say the longer you cook this kaddhi, the better the taste.

KADDHI (Parsi)

Cooking time:
40 minutes

1½ tablespoons of gram flour
2 cups of yoghurt
3 cups of water
1 large onion (chunky pieces, chopped length ways)
1¼ teaspoons of salt
¼ cup green coriander leaves (chopped)

Baghaar

1 tablespoon of butter/ghee
½ teaspoon of mustard seeds
2 fresh green chillies (whole or split length ways)
6 - 8 curry leaves

Mix the gram flour, salt, yoghurt and water making sure there are no lumps left in the mixture.

Heat ghee/butter in a good size pot and add the mustard seeds. When they pop, add chillies, curry leaves and onions. Stir for a few seconds and add the liquid mix. Leaving it on a high flame, keep stirring the mixture until it boils (ensuring no lumps form). Cook on a low heat for 25 to 30 minutes. (Its consistency should be between a thick and a thin soup)

Before serving add the coriander.

This kaddhi is quite tart in taste but I love the pieces of onions
infused with various flavours and the sourness of the yoghurt.

KADDHI (Sindhi)

Cooking time: 40
minutes

2 tablespoons of gram flour
3 - 4 tablespoons of tamarind paste
3 cups of water
16 - 20 bhindi (both ends snipped)
¼ teaspoon of turmeric
¼ teaspoon of chilli powder
1 teaspoon of salt
½ teaspoon of sugar
¼ cup of green coriander leaves (chopped)
oil for frying/grilling

Baghaar

1 tablespoon of butter/ghee
½ teaspoon of mustard seeds
2 dry red whole chillies

Deep fry or brush with oil and grill the bhindi.

On a very gentle heat, in a shallow pan, dry roast the gram flour until browned. When the flour is cold, mix in with all the spices, tamarind and water, making sure there are no lumps left in the mixture.

Heat ghee/butter in a good size pot and add the mustard seeds. When they pop, add whole chillies and the mixture. Leaving it on a high flame, keep stirring the mixture until it comes to the boil (ensuring no lumps form). Cook on a low heat for 20 to 25 minutes. Add bhindi and cook for another 5 minutes.

Before serving, add the coriander.

Bhindi can be substituted with green beans.

This, like the Punjabi kaddhi, is a bit intricate but really worth the bother. Again, courtesy of our Sindhi neighbours, I first tried this when I was about 10 or 11 years old and loved the taste of bhindi soaked in tart liquid and the liquid itself steeped in subtle flavours.

MASOOR DAL (Plain)

Cooking time:
20 minutes

1 cup of masoor dal
(washed and soaked in 3 cups of water)
½ teaspoon of coriander powder
¼ teaspoon of turmeric
¼ teaspoon of chilli powder
¾ teaspoon of salt
4 - 5 tablespoons of lemon juice

Baghaar

1 tablespoon of ghee or butter
½ teaspoon of cumin seeds
½ teaspoon of asafoetida powder

Bring the dal to boil and remove the froth that forms at the top. Add coriander, turmeric and chillies. Lower heat and simmer for 10 to 15 minutes (until soft and mushy).

Add salt and lemon juice and mix well (the consistency should be like a thick soup, therefore add water if necessary). Simmer for 2 to 3 minutes and take it off the heat.

Heat the ghee/butter in a small pan or bowl and add cumin seeds and asafoetida. As soon as these brown turn the heat off. Spread the mixture evenly on top of the cooked dal, gently stir and serve.

Whole Masoor (Plain) can be cooked in exactly the same way as Masoor dal.

Plain dals are always a delight with rice or rotis. They are delicate in taste and although cooked in same style they have their distinct individual flavours. Masoor dal takes the least time to boil. So, if rushed, this is the best one to go for.

MASOOR DAL (Bengali)

Cooking time:
25 minutes

**1 cup of masoor dal
(washed and soaked in 3 cups of water)
1 teaspoon of coriander powder
½ teaspoon of turmeric
½ teaspoon of cumin seeds
½ cup of onion (chopped)
1 to 2 green chillies (chopped)
¾ teaspoon of salt**

Baghaar

**2 tablespoons of ghee or butter
1½ tablespoons of garlic (finely chopped)**

Bring the dal to boil and remove the froth that forms at the top. Add coriander, turmeric, chillies, cumin and onions. Lower heat and simmer for 10 to 15 minutes (until soft and mushy). Add salt and mix well (the consistency should be like a thick soup, therefore add water if necessary). Simmer for 2 to 3 minutes and take it off the heat.

Heat ghee/butter in a small pan/bowl. Add garlic. As soon as it browns, turn the heat off. Spread the mixture evenly on top of the cooked dal, gently stir and serve.

I once worked with a group of Bangladeshi girls in North London to build their sense of self and self-confidence . To achieve this, amongst other approaches, I also organised cooking sessions. This meant that sometimes the girls would cook Bangladeshi vegetarian food for me and the other youthworker. For their age (10 to 14), they were very skilled in cookery. Sitting together with them, laughing, joking and polishing off the superb dishes they had prepared is a memory that vividly comes back to me every time I cook this dal that I learnt from them.

MASOOR DAL WITH COCONUT AND SPINACH
(South Indian style)

Cooking time:
25 minutes

½ cup of masoor dal
(washed and soaked in 2 cups of water)
½ teaspoon of coriander powder
1 teaspoon of sambhar powder *
¾ teaspoon of salt
4 tablespoons of coconut cream
1 cup of spinach (cooked)

Baghaar

2 tablespoons of oil
½ teaspoon of mustard seeds
½ stalk of leak or 1 medium onion
(chopped into medium pieces)
4 - 6 garlic pods (peeled)

* If ready sambhar powder is not
available, then substitute with:
1 tablespoon of fenugreek and coriander
seeds roasted and powdered, ¼ teaspoon
chilli powder and ¼ teaspoon turmeric.

Bring the dal to boil and remove the froth that forms at the top. Lower heat and simmer for 10 minutes (or until soft).

Heat oil in a pan and add the mustard seeds. As soon as these pop, add the curry leaves, garlic pod and leek/onion.

Toss around for a minute and stir in coconut, sambhar powder and coriander powder. Cook for another minute. Mix in the dal, spinach and salt. Cook on low heat for 5 to 6 minutes. The dish should have the consistency of a thick soup, therefore add water if necessary.

Serve with rice, dosa or idli.

This dish is a slightly simpler version of masoor dal with coconut and vegetables I once created with leftover dal. The family found it so appetizing that it has now become a regular part of my repertoire.

MOONG DAL (Plain)

Cooking time:
25 minutes

1 cup of moong dal
(washed and soaked in 4 cups of water)
½ teaspoon of coriander powder
¼ teaspoon of turmeric
¼ teaspoon of chilli powder
¾ teaspoon of salt
4 - 5 tablespoons of lemon juice

Baghaar

1 tablespoon of ghee or butter
½ teaspoon of cumin seeds
½ teaspoon of asafoetida powder

Bring the dal to boil and remove the froth that forms at the top. Add coriander, turmeric and chillies. Lower heat and simmer for 15 to 20 minutes (or until soft and mushy).

Add salt and lemon juice and mix well (the consistency should be like a thick soup, therefore add water if necessary). Simmer for 2 to 3 minutes and take it off the heat.

Heat ghee/butter in a small pan, add cumin seeds and asafoetida. As soon as these brown, turn the heat off. Spread the mixture evenly on top of the cooked dal, gently stir and serve.

This is one of the easiest dals to digest and is often given to recuperating patients for this reason, and also for its nourishing qualities.

MOONG DAL WITH COCONUT AND TOMATOES (Maharasthran)

Cooking time:
30 minutes

¾ cup of moong dal
(washed and soaked in 2 cups of water)
¾ teaspoon of coriander powder
¼ teaspoon of turmeric
¼ teaspoon of chilli powder
1 teaspoon of salt
4 - 5 tablespoons of lemon juice
1 teaspoon of sugar
1 teaspoon of fresh ginger (finely crushed)
1 teaspoon of garlic (finely crushed)
¼ cup of grated coconut (fresh or dry)
2 medium tomatoes (chopped small)
¼ cup green coriander leaves (chopped)

Baghaar

1 tablespoon of ghee or butter
½ teaspoon of cumin seeds
½ teaspoon of mustard seeds
½ teaspoon of asafoetida powder
4 cinnamon pieces (small)
4 cloves
6 - 8 curry leaves

Bring the dal to boil and remove the froth that forms at the top. Add coriander, turmeric and chillies. Lower heat and simmer for 15 to 20 minutes (or until soft and mushy).

Add salt, sugar, lemon juice, ginger, garlic, coconut and tomatoes. Mix well (the consistency should be akin to thin soup therefore add water accordingly). Simmer for 2 to 3 minutes and take it off the heat.

Heat ghee/butter in a small pan or bowl. Add cumin and mustard seeds and as soon as they pop add cloves, cinnamon and asafoetida. Stir for a few seconds then add the curry leaves and turn the heat off. Spread the mixture evenly on top of the cooked dal and gently stir in.

Before serving, sprinkle with green coriander.

I tasted this dal for the very first time when my grandmother was being treated for cancer in a Mumbai hospital. My naniji of course would not eat it because of the garlic and gave it to us children who were visiting her. (The hospital later ensured that she was given food without onion and garlic). I just loved the essence of all the spices, especially cinnamon, and the soothing soupy taste.

WHOLE MOONG WITH GARAM MASALA

Cooking time:
30 minutes

1 cup of moong (washed and soaked in 4 cups of water)
1 teaspoon of coriander powder
¼ teaspoon of turmeric
¼ teaspoon of crushed chilli
1 medium onion (chopped small)
1 tablespoon of ginger (chopped fine)
¾ teaspoon of salt

Baghaar

2 tablespoons of ghee or butter
½ teaspoon of cumin seeds
½ teaspoon of garam masala
1 tablespoon of garlic (finely crushed or chopped)

Add coriander, turmeric, chillies, onions and ginger to dal and bring it to boil. Lower heat and simmer for 15 to 20 minutes (until soft and mushy). Add salt and mix well (the consistency should be like a thick soup, therefore add water if necessary). Simmer for 2 to 3 minutes and take it off the heat.

Heat ghee/butter in a small pan. Add cumin seeds and when they have browned mix in garlic. Add garam masala and turn the heat off. Spread the mixture evenly on top of the cooked dal, gently stir and serve.

Our family friend Gurbir was a wonderful cook. We visited him in Germany where he lived for some years. He thrilled us with finger licking food throughout our visit. Besides some wonderful memories of travel around Germany, the recipe for this dal also came back with me.

WHOLE MOONG WITH YOGHURT (Gujarati)

Cooking time:
35 - 40 minutes

1 cup of moong
(washed and soaked in 4 cups of water)
1 teaspoon of coriander powder
½ teaspoon of turmeric
¼ teaspoon of chilli powder
1 tablespoon of ginger (paste)
1 tablespoon of garlic (paste)
1 cup of plain yoghurt
1 teaspoon of salt
¼ cup green coriander leaves (chopped)

Baghaar

1 tablespoon of ghee or butter
½ teaspoon of mustard seeds
1 medium onion (chopped small)
6 - 8 curry leaves

Add coriander, turmeric and chillies to moong and bring it to boil. Lower heat and simmer for 15 to 20 minutes (until soft).

Add salt, ginger and garlic. Mix in the yoghurt (the consistency should be between thick and thin soup, therefore add water if necessary). Simmer for 2 to 3 minutes and take it off the heat.

Heat ghee/butter in a small pan or bowl and add mustard seeds. As soon as these start to pop, add onions and fry until translucent. Add the curry leaves and the cooked moong, mix well and leave to cook on low heat for 5 minutes.

Before serving, sprinkle with green coriander.

I am always partial to Gujarati food, having first tasted it in Mumbai. But being part of a Gujarati family in London, I started picking up recipes from my Gujarati friends and also learning from my mother-in-law and her sister. To my family's delight, soon it became second nature for me to cook proper Gujarati meals just the way they liked.

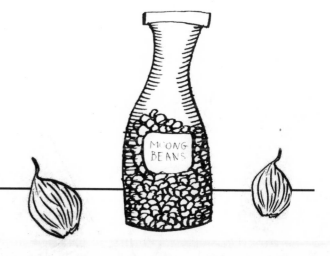

SPROUTED MOONG WITH GARLIC (Sindhi)

Cooking time:
15 minutes

2 cups of sprouted moong
½ teaspoon of coriander powder
¼ teaspoon of turmeric
¼ teaspoon of chilli powder
OR chopped green chilli
½ teaspoon of salt
½ cup of water
¼ cup of green coriander leaves (chopped)

Baghaar

2 tablespoons of oil
½ teaspoon of mustard seeds
1 tablespoon of garlic (paste)

Heat oil in a frying pan and add mustard seeds. As soon as these start to pop, add garlic and fry until golden brown. Add moong and all other spices. Add water and mix well. Cover and leave to cook on very low heat for 5 to 7 minutes.

Serve sprinkled with green coriander.

This dish can be made without garlic:
Substitute garlic with 2 to 3 spoons of lemon juice and cumin seeds for mustard.

This recipe again is from a Sindhi friend. I love its strong garlic flavour and its chewiness.

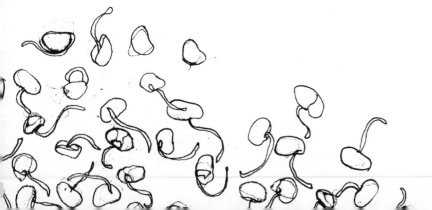

SPROUTED MOONG WITH COCONUT (Maharashtran)

Cooking time:
15 minutes

2 cups of sprouted moong
½ teaspoon of coriander powder
¼ teaspoon of turmeric
¼ teaspoon of chilli powder
¾ teaspoon of salt
½ cup of water
¼ cup of green coriander leaves (chopped)

Baghaar

2 tablespoons of oil
½ teaspoon of mustard seeds
1 medium onion (chopped small)
1 tablespoon of garlic (finely chopped)
½ cup of grated coconut (fresh or dry)
6 - 8 curry leaves

Heat oil in a frying pan, add mustard seeds and as soon as these start to pop, add onions and fry until transparent. Add garlic and curry leaves. Put in all the other spices plus the coconut, fry for a minute.

Add moong and water and mix well. Cover and leave to cook on a very low heat for 5 to 7 minutes.

Before serving, sprinkle with green coriander.

This recipe is not that dissimilar to the Sindhi one but the coconut adds that extra taste to the dish.

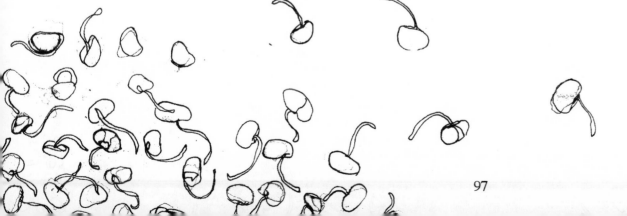

RED KIDNEY BEANS (Plain)

Cooking time:
40 minutes

**1 cup of kidney beans ready
(washed and soaked in 5 cups of water)
OR 800g tinned
1 teaspoon of coriander powder
½ teaspoon of turmeric
¼ teaspoon of crushed chilli
1 teaspoon of salt
1 - 2 tablespoons fresh tamarind paste
OR 1 - 2 tablespoons of tomato puree
1 tablespoon of ginger (finely chopped)
¼ cup of green coriander leaves (chopped)**

Baghaar

**2 tablespoons of ghee / butter
½ teaspoon of cumin seeds
½ teaspoon of asafoetida**

Bring the beans to boil. Lower heat and simmer for 25 to 30 minutes (or until soft). (A pressure cooker can boil them in about 7 minutes)

Add salt and tamarind. Simmer for 2 to 3 minutes (there should be enough liquid to cover the beans therefore add water if necessary) and take it off the heat. If using tinned beans, simply add the tamarind and also reduce the amount of salt.

Heat ghee / butter in a pan. Add cumin seeds and asafoetida. As soon as these brown, add coriander, turmeric, and chilli powder and stir for a few seconds (if using tomato puree, add it now and cook for a minute).

Mix in the cooked beans with liquid and let the mixture simmer for 10 to 15 minutes. Sprinkle green coriander and serve.

My last trip to India was very exciting and emotional as the whole family had gathered from different corners of the world for my niece's wedding. Together with my siblings I went to visit my chachaji (uncle) in Deheradun, my father's home town. This is one of the dishes that my chachiji (aunt) fed us, flooding back memories of childhood and delicious family meals.

RED KIDNEY BEANS (with Onions)

Cooking time:
45 minutes

1 cup kidney beans (washed and soaked in 5 cups of water)
OR ready cooked 800g tin
1 teaspoon of coriander powder
½ teaspoon of garam masala
¼ teaspoon of turmeric
¼ teaspoon of crushed chilli
1¼ teaspoons of salt
1 - 2 tablespoons of fresh tamarind paste
OR 1 - 2 tablespoons of tomato puree
¼ cup of green coriander leaves (chopped)

Baghaar

2 tablespoons of ghee / butter
½ teaspoon of cumin seeds
1 large onion (finely chopped)
1 tablespoon of ginger (finely chopped)
1 tablespoon of garlic (finely chopped)

Bring the beans to boil. Lower heat and simmer for 25 to 30 minutes (or until soft). (A pressure cooker can boil them in about 7 minutes)

Add salt and tamarind. Simmer for 2 to 3 minutes (there should be enough liquid to cover the beans therefore add water if necessary) and take it off the heat. If using tinned beans, simply add the tamarind and reduce the amount of salt.

Heat ghee / butter in a pan, add cumin seeds and, as soon as these brown, add onions. Fry until golden, add garlic and, stir for few seconds. Add coriander, turmeric, garam masala and chilli powder and stir for another few seconds (if using tomato puree, add it now and cook for a minute).

Mix in the cooked beans with liquid and let the mixture simmer for 10 to 15 minutes. (The dish should have some gravy) Sprinkle green coriander and serve.

½ cup of fried (or grilled) paneer cubes can be added to the above along with extra chilli and salt. Reduce the amount of beans appropriately.

This is the Punjabi version of the previous recipe which I picked up from Punjabi neighbours in Mumbai. This has a richer taste and is just delectable with rice.

TOOR/ARHAR DAL (Plain)

Cooking time:
25 minutes

**1 cup of toor dal
(washed and soaked in 3 cups of water)
½ teaspoon of coriander powder
¼ teaspoon of turmeric
¼ teaspoon of chilli powder
¾ teaspoon of salt
3 - 4 tablespoons of lemon juice**

Baghaar

**1 tablespoon of ghee or butter
½ teaspoon of cumin seeds
½ teaspoon of asafoetida powder**

Bring the dal to boil and remove the froth that forms at the top. Add coriander, turmeric and chillies. Lower heat and simmer for 15 to 20 minutes (or until soft and mushy).

Add salt and lemon juice and mix well (the consistency should be between thick and thin soup therefore add water if necessary). Simmer for 2 to 3 minutes and take it off the heat.

Heat ghee/butter in a small pan or bowl. Add cumin seeds and asafoetida. As soon as these brown, turn the heat off. Spread the mixture evenly on top of the cooked dal, gently stir and serve.

This dish can be made with garlic. Use a bit of extra ghee in baghaar and, after cumin seeds have browned, add 2 tablespoons of finely chopped garlic.

Although the dals or beans cooked at home in India varied from season to season and from day to day, I absolutely enjoyed them all. But the plain arhar dal remains my favourite. To this day when I am tired and hungry all I desire is this dal, rice and some pickle.

TOOR DAL (Gujarati)

Cooking time:
30 minutes

1 cup of toor dal
(washed and soaked in 3 cups of water)
½ teaspoon of coriander powder
¼ teaspoon of turmeric
¼ teaspoon of chilli powder
1 teaspoon of salt
3 - 4 tablespoons of lemon juice
1 tablespoon of crushed ginger
1 tablespoon of crushed garlic (optional)
1 tablespoon of sugar
1 medium tomato (chopped small)
2 - 4 green chillies sliced length wise (optional)
6 - 8 curry leaves
¼ cup of green coriander leaves (chopped)

Baghaar

1 tablespoon of ghee or butter
¼ teaspoon of mustard seeds
¼ teaspoon of fenugreek seeds
¼ teaspoon of cumin seeds
½ teaspoon of asafoetida powder
(omit this if using garlic)

Bring the dal to the boil and remove the froth that forms at the top. Add coriander, turmeric and chillies. Lower heat and simmer for 15 to 20 minutes (or until soft and mushy).

Add salt, curry leaves, lemon juice, sugar, ginger and garlic and mix well (the consistency should be between thick and thin soup, therefore, add water accordingly). Simmer for 5 minutes, add tomato and take it off the heat.

Heat ghee/butter in a small pan/bowl. Add mustard and fenugreek seeds and as soon as they pop, add cumin seeds and asafoetida. As soon as these brown, turn the heat off. Spread the mixture evenly on top of the cooked dal, gently stir and sprinkle green coriander and chillies and serve.

This is a delicious concoction, full of delicate flavours and goes down a treat as a soupy drink, especially in the winter months.

TOOR DAL DHANSAK (Parsi)

Cooking time:
40 minutes

¾ cup of toor dal
(washed and soaked in 3 cups of water)
1½ teaspoons of coriander powder
¼ teaspoon of turmeric
¼ teaspoon of chilli powder
1 teaspoon of salt
1 medium tomato (chopped)
1 small aubergine (chopped)
1 medium onion chopped
1 small carrot (copped)
1 green chilli (chopped)

Baghaar

2 tablespoons of ghee or butter
½ teaspoon of cumin seeds
2 tablespoons of garlic (crushed)
1 tablespoon of ginger (crushed)
½ teaspoon of garam masala

Bring the dal to boil and remove the froth that forms at the top. Add coriander, turmeric and chillies. Lower heat and simmer for 15 to 20 minutes (or until soft and mushy).

Add all the vegetables and salt and simmer until soft and mushy. With a heavy ladle, mash up the vegetables so that they are well mixed in with the dal. Simmer for 5 minutes and take it off the heat (the consistency should be like a thick soup, therefore add water if necessary).

Heat ghee/butter in a small pan or bowl and add cumin seeds. As soon as these brown, add garlic, ginger and garam masala and fry for half a minute. Turn the heat off. Spread the mixture evenly on top of the cooked dal, gently stir and serve.

My Parsi friend Katie's mother, used to cook this to perfection - a meal in itself of vegetables and dal. She used to serve this with a vegetable (cauliflower or beans or aubergines) cooked in coconut and with boiled rice. What bliss!

SAMBHAR (South Indian)

Cooking time:
40 minutes

¾ cup of toor dal
(washed and soaked in 3 cups of water)
1 teaspoon of coriander powder
¼ teaspoon of turmeric
¼teaspoon of chilli powder
1 teaspoon of salt
1 small aubergine
(sliced in cubes - approx. 12 pieces)
1 medium onion chopped
(sliced thick lengthwise)
2 whole green chillies
2 - 3 teaspoons of tamarind paste
6 - 8 curry leaves
½ teaspoon of fenugreek seeds
(dry roasted and ground rough)
1 teaspoon of coriander seeds
(dry roasted and ground rough)

(if ready made sambhar powder is at
hand then use 1 teaspoon of that and
omit chilli and turmeric)

Baghaar

1 tablespoon of ghee or butter
½ teaspoon of cumin seeds
½ teaspoon of mustard seeds
½ teaspoon of asafoetida

Bring the dal to boil and remove the froth that forms at the top. Add coriander, turmeric and chilli powder. Lower heat and simmer for 15 to 20 minutes (or until soft and mushy).

Heat the ghee/butter in a good sized pan. Add cumin and mustard seeds, as soon as these brown, add asafoetida. Give it a few seconds and stir in the vegetables, green chillies and curry leaves (if using sambhar powder add now) and cook until vegetables are soft.

Mix in salt and the roasted, powdered fenugreek and coriander seeds, tamarind and the cooked dal (the consistency of the sambhar should be on the thin side – but not watery - therefore add water if necessary). Simmer 5 to 7 minutes and then take it off the heat.

Although nowadays sambhar powder is easily available in most South Asian grocery shops, when I first learned this dish from my friend Prema's mother, one had to prepare the extra mixture of roasted fenugreek, coriander seeds and powder them oneself. Even when using sambhar powder I still use this mixture for additional aroma. Over the years, with my move to UK, I have sadly lost contact with Prema. So Prema by any chance if you come across this book please do get in touch.

URAD DAL (Plain)

Cooking time:
20 minutes

1 cup of urad dal (washed and soaked in 3 cups of water)
1 teaspoon of coriander powder
¼ teaspoon of turmeric
¼ teaspoon of crushed chilli
¾ teaspoon of salt
1 tablespoon of fresh ginger (finely chopped)

Baghaar

1 tablespoon of ghee or butter
½ teaspoon of cumin seeds
½ teaspoon of asafoetida powder
OR 1 tablespoon of garlic (finely chopped)
½ teaspoon of garam masala

Bring the dal to boil and remove the froth that forms at the top. Add coriander and chilli. Lower heat and simmer for 10 to 15 minutes (until soft but not mushy). Add salt and ginger. (The consistency should be like a thick soup). Simmer for 2 to 3 minutes and take it off the heat.

Heat ghee/butter in a small pan or bowl. Add cumin seeds, garlic or asafoetida. As soon as these brown, add garam masala and turn the heat off. Spread the mixture evenly on top of the cooked dal, gently stir and serve.

It is important not to overcook this dal as it turns into one sticky mush.

It goes equally well with rice or roti.

URAD DAL (with Tomatoes)

Cooking time:
35 minutes

1 cup of urad dal
(washed and soaked in 2 cups of water)
1 teaspoon of coriander powder
¼ teaspoon of crushed chilli
¾ teaspoon of salt
1 tablespoon of fresh ginger
(finely chopped)

Baghaar

2 tablespoons of ghee or butter
½ teaspoon of cumin seeds
1 tablespoon of garlic (finely chopped)
2 medium tomatoes (finely chopped)

Bring the dal to boil and remove the froth that forms at the top. Add coriander, turmeric and chillies. Lower heat and simmer for 8 to 10 minutes (dal should be soft but still with a bite) and dry out the water to minimum. Add salt and ginger, mix well, simmer for 2 to 3 minutes and take it off the heat.

Heat ghee/butter in a small pan/bowl. Add cumin seeds. As soon as these brown, add garlic and fry until golden. Mix in tomatoes and cook for a minute. Turn the heat off. Spread the mixture evenly on top of the cooked dal, gently stir and serve.

My dad was very fond of good food and took delight in searching out good places for the best dishes. We would at times travel right across the city for some special food place or dish. Like real food lovers, he didn't care about upmarket/ trendy places. His main focus was food - ambience and status being the icing on the cake. He tried out urad dal cooked in this particular way in one of the Mumbai dhabbas and loved it. Since by this time I was the daring cook in the family, I reproduced it as per my dad's instructions. To my joy he was more than pleased with the result.

WHOLE URAD (Plain)

Cooking time:
40 minutes

1 cup of urad dal
(washed and soaked in 5 cups of water)
1 teaspoon of coriander powder
¼ teaspoon of turmeric
¼ teaspoon of crushed chilli
¾ teaspoon of salt
1 tablespoon of fresh ginger (finely chopped)

Baghaar

1 tablespoon of ghee or butter
½ teaspoon of cumin seeds
½ teaspoon of asafoetida powder

Bring the dal to boil and remove the froth that forms at the top. Add coriander, and chillies. Lower heat and simmer for 30 to 35 minutes (until soft but not mushy).

Add salt and ginger and mix well (the consistency should be like a thick soup therefore add water if necessary). Simmer for 2 to 3 minutes and take it off the heat.

Heat ghee/butter in a small pan/bowl. Add cumin seeds and asafoetida. Spread the mixture evenly on top of the cooked dal, gently stir and serve.

To weed out the small shiny hard bits that look very much like the dal itself, soak the dal. This will soften the dal making it easier to identify the hard bits. Put the small amounts of soaked dal on a plate and go through it carefully to pick out the culprits.

My first memory of eating this dal goes back to when I must have been 5 or 6. It was the day of Holi festival when everyone throws coloured powder or liquid at each other. All barriers between young and old, rich and poor, men and women are forgotten and all make as much mess as possible of others with wet and dry colours. So, having played Holi in the morning part and all cleaned up, my mother sat the family down for lunch of urad dal, rice and vegetables. I still remember my wonderment at the combination of colours - the black dal and white basmati rice. The two together were not only picture perfect but also created a most irresistible bouquet. A feast for more than mere taste buds!

WHOLE URAD (with Onions)

Cooking time:
45 minutes

1 cup of urad
(washed and soaked in 5 cups of water)
1 teaspoon of coriander powder
¼ teaspoon of turmeric
¼ teaspoon of crushed chilli
¾ teaspoon of salt
1 tablespoon of fresh ginger (finely chopped)
1 tablespoon of garlic (finely chopped)
2 bay leaves
2 tablespoons of thick cream (optional)

Baghaar

3 tablespoons of ghee or butter
½ teaspoon of cumin seeds
1 medium onion (finely chopped)

Bring the dal to boil and remove the froth that forms at the top. Add coriander, turmeric and chillies. Lower heat and simmer for 30 to 35 minutes (until soft but not mushy).

Add salt, ginger and garlic. Mix well (the consistency should be like a thick soup therefore add water if necessary). Simmer for 2 to 3 minutes and take it off the heat.

Heat ghee/butter in a small pan or bowl and add cumin seeds. As soon as these brown, add onions and fry until golden. Mix this into the dal and cook on low heat for for a minute or two. Before serving, mix in the cream.

Optional: you can mix in a ¼ cup of cooked red kidney beans along with the salt etc. This gives a nice colour to the dish.

This dal is simply yummy with extra ghee spread on top.

DAL SPECIAL

Cooking time:
45 minutes

**1 cup mix of dals - urad dal, whole moong, chana dal, whole masoor & toor dal, all in equal quantities
(washed and soaked in 5 cups of water)
1 teaspoon of coriander powder
¼ teaspoon of turmeric
¼ teaspoon of crushed chilli
¾ teaspoon of salt
2 tablespoons of fennel seeds
2 tablespoons of fresh ginger (finely chopped)**

Baghaar

**2 tablespoons of ghee or butter
½ teaspoon of cumin seeds
1 medium onion (finely chopped)
1 tablespoon of garlic (finely chopped)**

Bring the dal to boil and remove the froth that forms at the top. Add ginger, fennel, coriander, turmeric and chillies. Lower heat and simmer for 25 - 30 minutes (or until soft but not mushy). Mix in salt (the consistency of dal should be like a thick soup, therefore add water if necessary). Simmer for 2 - 3 minutes and take it off the heat.

Heat ghee/butter in a small pan or bowl and add cumin seeds. As soon as these brown, add onions and fry until golden. Mix in garlic. Turn the heat off. Spread the mixture evenly on top of the cooked dal and gently stir it in.

My niece Rashmi, who, like me, loves to cook, lived in Singapore for a while. Being a very outgoing person, she promptly made friends with a number of people - amongst them a few families from different parts of India. And also being a foody, no sooner had she befriended someone than she elicited a recipe from them. Amongst the many recipes she sent me, this one from Himachal Pradesh in Northen India, was not only new to me but also very tasty. This obviously is a well travelled recipe that has, it seems, pleased all who have tried it.

Vegetables

Vegetables need no introduction - their variety unending and each one unique in taste, shape, colour and properties. They are rich in minerals, vitamins, roughage and everything that is good for our health and wellbeing. The vegetables I have used in my recipes are readily available in most areas of the UK. Vegetables such as aubergine have been available in local supermarkets and grocers for quite some time. But, some of them are now also stocking vegetables like lauki and bhindi.

Tips:

- Wash all vegetables before chopping. This way they lose less of their vitamins and minerals.

- Most vegetables such as marrow, courgettes, aubergine do not need to be peeled unless otherwise specified.

- Lauki needs to be scraped only.

- To get a crispy drier feel to bhindi, wash and then dry them before cutting to the required size.

- If you wish to keep water based vegetables such as courgettes, bhindi, marrow and cauliflower crispy or firm do not add salt at the beginning of the cooking process.

- The leaves of cauliflower, if tender, can be used within a specific recipe or taken off and used to make a separate vegetable.

- I have included paneer recipes in the vegetable section a) because most of them require the inclusion of a vegetable, and b) because they are treated as complementary dishes with dals and beans.

- Except potatoes and cauliflower (both of which loose their texture), most leftover vegetables can be frozen or extra amounts can be cooked to freeze and store.

Baigun - Aubergine (Also known as egg-plant and Brinjal).

At our home in Mumbai aubergine was the most commonly cooked vegetable as it was cheap and available all year round. We children would scream "NOT AGAIN" every time our mother served up aubergine in yet another form. But in the UK it became a luxury and I did learn to value it much more. Although rich in potassium and folic acid, baigun (this name is used in most Sanskrit based Indian languages), means 'one without qualities'. However, all said and done, it is a tasty and versatile vegetable with an alluring colour and shape. Its size varies from one weighing almost 400 to 500 grams to baby ones of 5 to 6 grams. For most recipes the large ones are quite appropriate but for the recipes that require stuffing one would use the baby ones.

Tips:

- If you are chopping the aubergines in advance it is best to leave them in a pan of water as they oxidize very quickly and go bitter. I tend to cut them at the last minute straight into the pot.

- At times when you need to cook only a portion of the vegetable and you want to keep the rest for later, the best way of stopping oxidization is to rub the exposed part with a small amount of turmeric (covering all the skinless area).

- It is not always easy to find small aubergines therefore one or two bigger ones can be used for 'stuffed' recipes, whereby the whole vegetable can be stuffed, cooked and cut into appropriate pieces when serving.

BAIGUN BHAJA

Cooking time:
15-20 minutes

½ kg aubergine
(chopped into medium size pieces)
1 medium potato
(peeled and chopped into 6 pieces)
1 teaspoon of coriander powder
¼ teaspoon of crushed chillies
¼ teaspoon of turmeric
½ teaspoon of salt
3 to 4 tablespoons of
lemon juice (optional)

Baghaar

6 tablespoons of oil
½ teaspoon of cumin seeds
½ teaspoon of asafoetida

Heat oil in a wok. Add cumin seeds and asafoetida. When browned, add potatoes and sauté for 2 to 3 minutes.

Add the aubergine and all other ingredients (except lemon juice). Stir well, cover and cook on a low heat for 3 to 4 minutes.

Stir the vegetables on a high heat for a few minutes until they turn crispy. Mix in lemon juice and serve.

This is the recipe which my mother fed to us most often. What a difference a few years (well actually many more than a few) make. The one time despair at the mere mention of this dish has now turned into a delightful anticipation.

PEELED AUBERGINE

Cooking time:
15 - 20 minutes

¾ kg aubergine
(peeled & chopped into medium size pieces)
1 teaspoon of coriander powder
¼ teaspoon of crushed chillies
½ teaspoon of salt

Baghaar

1 tablespoon of butter/ghee
½ teaspoon of cumin seeds
½ teaspoon of fenugreek
½ teaspoon of asafoetida

Heat ghee/butter in a wok. Add fenugreek seeds and, when they pop, add cumin seeds and asafoetida. When browned, add aubergines and all other ingredients.

Stir well, cover and cook on a low heat for 5 to 7 minutes, turning it around once or twice. Ensure that the vegetable is not too dry and add a spoon or two of water if necessary.

Two spoons of yoghurt can be added (with extra salt) for additional taste and flavour.

My aunt in Deheradun cooked this dish the best. She served it with seven layered parathas – each layer could be neatly separated. It was a perfect combination of squishy vegetable, with oozing-with-aroma parathas. The outer layers were so crispy and the inner layers would simply melt in your mouth.

AUBERGINE WITH PIGEON PEAS (Gujarati)

Cooking time:
15-20 minutes

½ kg aubergine (chopped into medium size pieces)
½ cup of pigeon peas
1 teaspoon of coriander powder
½ teaspoon of cumin powder
¼ teaspoon of chilli powder
¼ teaspoon of turmeric
¾ teaspoon of salt
¼ teaspoon of sugar
¼ cup of green coriander leaves (chopped)

Baghaar

3 tablespoons of oil
1 teaspoon of mustard seeds
½ teaspoon of asafoetida
6 to 8 curry leaves

Heat oil in a pan. Add mustard seeds, when they pop add asafoetida followed by the curry leaves. When browned, add aubergine, peas and all the other spices.

Stir well, cover and cook on low heat for 5 to 7 minutes turning it around once or twice. Ensure the vegetable is not too dry and add a spoon or two of water if necessary.

Before serving, garnish with coriander.

I don't know about the pigeons but I do like this combination – the soft vegetable, with a touch of sweetness and the peas still firm, with a bite to them. This dish goes best with thin rotis.

AUBERGINE SLICES WITH CHILLI AND LEMON

Cooking time:
15-20 minutes

1 kg aubergine
(chopped into round slices 10 to 12 pieces)
¼ teaspoon of crushed or powdered chillies
½ teaspoon of salt
2 - 3 tablespoons of lemon juice
8 - 10 tablespoons of oil

Heat half the oil in a large frying pan and place the aubergine pieces in the pan. While these are cooking, brush the top side of each piece with the remaining oil and shallow fry them on both sides on low to medium heat until crisp on the outside and soft inside (alternatively you can also brush both side of the slices with oil and grill them).

Before serving, if required, warm the slices again and sprinkle with salt, chilli and lemon juice.

This serves equally well as an accompaniment with drinks, or as a starter with some side salads, or as a vegetable as part of the main meal.

AUBERGINE STUFFED (North Indian)

Cooking time:
15-20 minutes

6 - 8 small (8 to 10 cm long) aubergines
3 teaspoons of coriander powder
¼ teaspoon of chilli powder
¼ teaspoon of turmeric
¾ teaspoon of salt
¼ teaspoon of sugar
3 - 4 tablespoons of lemon juice

Baghaar

4 tablespoons of oil
½ teaspoon of cumin seeds
½ teaspoon of asafoetida

Carefully make an incision (lengthways) in each aubergine so as not to cut them apart at the top or bottom. Mix all the spices and lemon juice together (if too dry add a spoon or two of water).

Divide the mixture roughly into 6 to 8 portions and stuff the aubergines.

Heat the oil in wok, add cumin seeds and asafoetida. When browned, add the aubergines.

Toss them around until they are well covered in oil, cover and cook on low heat for 4 to 5 minutes (turning the aubergines over once or twice). Remove the lid and leave roasting on a very low heat (and turning from time to time) until the skin turns nice and crispy.

The trick with this one is to cook it without breaking the vegetable. Some people tie the aubergines with thread to avoid this. But, you really don't need to worry about 'stringing' them, if you cook them in a flat frying pan, do not pack them in too tight and are careful when turning each aubergine. The dish goes very well with parathas.

AUBERGINE STUFFED (Parsee)

Cooking time:
20 - 25 minutes

6 - 8 small (8 to 10 cm long) aubergines
4 tablespoons of coconut powder or
fresh grated coconut
1 - 1½ tablespoons of tamarind paste
1 teaspoon of coriander powder
¼ teaspoon of chilli powder
¼ teaspoon of turmeric
1 teaspoon of salt
¼ teaspoon of sugar
1 tablespoon of garlic (paste)

Baghaar

6 tablespoons of oil
½ teaspoon of mustard seeds

Carefully make an incision (lengthways) in each aubergine so as not to cut them apart at the top or bottom. Mix all the spices, coconut and tamarind together (if too dry add a spoon or two of water). Divide the mixture roughly into 6 to 8 portions and stuff the aubergines.

Heat oil in a wok. Add mustard seeds and, when they pop, add the aubergines. Toss them around until they are well covered in oil.

Cover and cook on low heat for 4 to 5 minutes (turning the aubergines over once or twice). Remove the lid and leave roasting on very low heat (and turning from time to time) until the skin turns nice and crispy.

When I first ate this at my friend Katie's house, I was totally bowled over. This is absolutely fantastic with rice and dal.

AUBERGINE STUFFED (Gujarati)

Cooking time:
20 - 25 minutes

6 - 8 small (8 to 10 cm long) aubergine
2 tablespoons of roasted peanuts
(crushed)
2 tablespoons of dry roasted gram flour
½ teaspoon of coriander powder
½ teaspoon of cumin powder
¼ teaspoon of chilli powder
¼ teaspoon of turmeric
3 - 4 tablespoons of lemon juice
¾ teaspoon of salt
¼ teaspoon of sugar
1 teaspoon of garlic

Baghaar

6 tablespoons oil
1 teaspoon of mustard seeds

Carefully make an incision (lengthwise) in each aubergine so as not to cut them apart at the top or bottom. Mix all the spices, gram flour, peanuts and lemon juice together (if too dry add a spoon or two of water). Divide the mixture roughly into 6 to 8 portions and stuff the aubergines.

Heat oil in a wok. Add mustard seeds and when they pop, add the vegetables. Toss them around until they are well covered in oil. Cover and cook on a medium heat for 5 to 7 minutes (turning them over once or twice).

Remove the lid and leave roasting on a very low heat (turning from time to time) until the skin turns nice and crispy.

Gujarati food provides a perfect blend of delicate flavours melded together in a meal but also often in one dish. I learnt this recipe from my friend Shobha who is a real whiz cook.

AUBERGINE WITH TOMATOES AND ONIONS (1)

Cooking time:
20 - 25 minutes

½ kg aubergine
(chopped into medium size pieces)
2 medium tomatoes
(chopped into 4 pieces each)
1 teaspoon of coriander powder
½ teaspoon of garam masala
¼ teaspoon of crushed chillies
¼ teaspoon of turmeric powder
¾ teaspoon of salt
¼ cup green coriander leaves (chopped)

Baghaar

4 tablespoons of oil
½ teaspoon of cumin seeds
1 large onion (chopped medium pieces)

Heat oil in a pan and add cumin seeds. As soon as they brown, add the onions and fry until nicely browned. Add all the other spices. Stir for few seconds.

Stir in the aubergine, add salt and cook (with lid on) on a low heat until the pieces are cooked but not mushy (5 to 7 minutes).

Add the tomatoes and stir for 1 to 2 minutes. Sprinkle with green coriander and serve.

The fennel in this gives the dish a distinct, slightly sweetish aroma. My best friend Prabha - another good cook - had often fed me this.

AUBERGINE WITH TOMATOES AND ONIONS (2)

Cooking time:
20 - 25 minutes

½ kg aubergine
(chopped into medium size pieces)
2 medium tomatoes
(chopped into 4 pieces each)
1 teaspoon of coriander powder
1 teaspoon of fennel powder
¼ teaspoon of crushed chillies
¼ teaspoon of turmeric powder
¾ teaspoon of salt
¼ cup green coriander leaves (chopped)

Baghaar

4 tablespoons of oil
½ teaspoon of cumin seeds
1 large onion (chopped medium pieces)

Heat oil in a pan and add cumin seeds. As soon as they brown, add the onions and fry until nicely browned. Add all the other spices. Stir for a few seconds. Add tomatoes and cook on a high heat until the liquid has evaporated.

Stir in the aubergine, add salt and cook (with the lid on) on low heat until the pieces are cooked but not mushy (5 to 7 minutes). Sprinkle green coriander and serve.

This dish, with its nice thick, very aromatic gravy, is absolutely perfect with parathas.

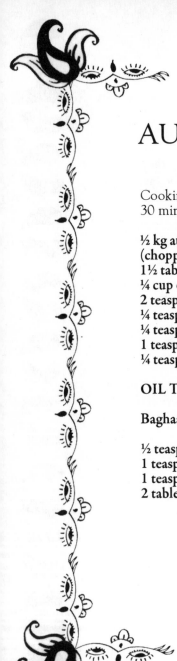

AUBERGINE IN TAMARIND SAUCE

Cooking time:
30 minutes

½ kg aubergine
(chopped into medium size pieces)
1½ tablespoons of tamarind pulp
¼ cup of water
2 teaspoons of coriander powder
¼ teaspoon of chilli powder
¼ teaspoon of turmeric powder
1 teaspoon of salt
¼ teaspoon of sugar

OIL TO DEEP FRYING

Baghaar

½ teaspoon of cumin seeds
1 teaspoon of garlic (paste)
1 teaspoon of ginger (paste)
2 tablespoons of green coriander (paste)

Deep fry the aubergine pieces in very hot oil (or coat with oil and grill until browned).

In a shallow pan put 1 tablespoon of oil and add cumin seeds. As soon as they brown, add ginger, garlic and green coriander paste, stir for few a seconds and add all other dry spices.

Stir in tamarind and water. Cook for 5 minutes on a low heat and gently mix in the fried aubergine. Simmer for a few minutes and serve.

In my long, varied life, I lived and worked for some years in Bangladesh and learned a few dishes there of which this one is my favourite. With my daughter, grandson and nephew who were visiting us, we took a boat trip to the Sunderbans – the mangrove region, the tiger land – in the southern-most part of Bangladesh. In this serene environment, the boat gliding gently, we watched the deer and other wild life (no sighting of the tigers though, except paw prints here and there). I managed to get the recipe for this dish (after having eaten it) from the organiser of the trip, an amazing woman, who had studied at Shantiniketan and had led a very interesting life (if you are reading this by any chance, please accept my thanks again for the recipe and for a wonderful trip).

BHARTA

Cooking time:
40 minutes

1 kg aubergine (whole)
1 teaspoon of oil
2 medium tomatoes
(chopped into 8 pieces each)
2 teaspoons of coriander powder
¼ teaspoon of crushed chillies
¼ teaspoon of turmeric powder
1 teaspoon of salt
1 teaspoon of garam masala (optional)
¼ cup green coriander leaves (chopped)

Baghaar

3 tablespoons of butter/ghee
½ teaspoon of cumin seeds
½ teaspoon of garlic (chopped fine)
1 tablespoon of ginger (chopped fine)
1 large onion (chopped fine)

Lightly brush the aubergine(s) with oil, make 1 or 2 small pricks in the skin and roast in a hot oven for about half an hour until the skin is charred and the inside is soft. When cold, peel and mash them.

Heat butter/ghee in a pan. Add cumin seeds. As soon as they brown, add the onions and fry until nicely browned. Add ginger, garlic and all the other spices (except garam masala). Stir for a few seconds and stir in the aubergine. Mix well and cook on gentle heat for 12 to 15 minutes (or until juices evaporate and ghee shows), turning it over every 2 to 3 minutes.

Add the tomatoes and cook for a further 2 to 3 minutes. Before serving, sprinkle the garam masala and coriander.

This is one of my favourite dishes - maybe because it needs lots of ghee to give it that extra taste. It takes time and effort but is definitely worth it. We (the family) once had our Sunday lunch at a Punjabi restaurant in Mumbai. Since we had not booked a table the proprietor, a friend of my dad's, set one up for us in the yard next to the kitchen. The aubergines were being roasted on a coalfire for bharta. The charred smell from them was just so enticing that needless to say we ordered bharta for our meal – one of the best I have had.

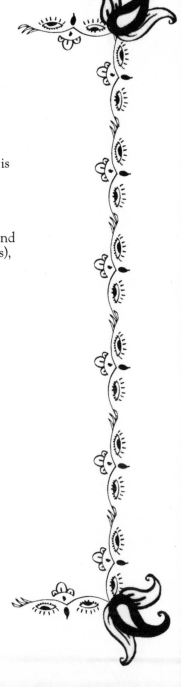

Bhindi (Okra / Ladies Fingers)

Bhindi, generally known in the west as okra or ladies fingers, is an interesting vegetable in that some people simply love it (like Gordon, my partner) cooked every way and some people hate it (like my son Rahul) because, it is a bit slimy. However, it is very commonly used not only in Indian, but also in Middle Eastern and Southern European cuisine.

CRISPY BHINDI

Cooking time:
15-20 minutes

½ kg bhindi
½ teaspoon of coriander powder
¼ teaspoon of crushed chillies
¼ teaspoon of turmeric
½ teaspoon of salt

Baghaar

3 tablespoons of oil
½ teaspoon of cumin seeds
½ teaspoon of asafoetida

Snip the top and the bottom of the bhindi and cut it into 3cm pieces. Heat oil in a wok. Add cumin seeds and asafoetida. When browned, add bhindi and all other ingredients except salt. Stir well and cook on low heat for 5 to 7 minutes.

Before serving, cook the bhindi on medium heat until browned and mix in the salt.

This dish can be cooked with yoghurt.
In the final stage, after bhindi has turned crisp, transfer it to a serving dish, pour 1 cup yoghurt and serve.

This version was cooked by our friend Chandra, who besides being a good doctor is also a very good cook.

This dish can be cooked with onions.
Chop 1 medium onion into small pieces. In the baghaar stage, instead of asafoetida, add the onion, toss it for a few seconds and then add bhindi.

This dish can also be cooked with potatoes.
Slice 1 medium potato, slightly bigger than bhindi. After the baghaar, add the potato cook for 3 to 4 minutes, then add the bhindi (add extra salt).

This is my nanaji's (grandmother) recipe. She was an amazing cook – never used onion or garlic but everything she prepared was scrumptious. I spent my early childhood in my grandparents' home in Baripada, a small town in Orissa. In my nanaji's kitchen only North Indian style and strictly vegetarian food was cooked. The food was cooked in very little oil or ghee, lightly spiced and therefore had subtle flavours and aromas. It was always extremely tasty, balanced and healthy.

BHINDI WITH LEMON

Cooking time:
15 minutes

½ kg bhindi (chopped into 2cm pieces)
1 teaspoon of coriander powder
¼ teaspoon of crushed chillies
¼ teaspoon of turmeric
½ teaspoon of salt
3 - 4 tablespoons lemon juice

Baghaar

2 tablespoons of oil
½ teaspoon of cumin seeds
½ teaspoon of asafoetida

Heat oil in a wok. Add cumin seeds and asafoetida. When browned, add bhindi and all other ingredients (except lemon juice).

Stir well, cover and cook on a low heat for 4 to 6 minutes. The vegetable should be dry (but not crispy). Sprinkle lemon juice, mix and serve.

This is also from my grandmother's repertoire, which my mother and I continue to follow.

BHINDI WITH TOMATO

Cooking time:
15 - 20 minutes

½ kg bhindi (snipped at the top and bottom)
2 medium tomatoes (chopped into small slices)
1 teaspoon of coriander powder
¼ teaspoon of crushed chillies
¼ teaspoon of turmeric
¾ teaspoon of salt
¼ cup green coriander leaves (chopped)

Baghaar

6 tablespoons of oil
½ teaspoon of cumin seeds
1 medium onion (chopped lengthways)

Heat oil in a pan. Add cumin seeds. As soon they brown, add the onions and fry until nicely browned.

Add all other spices. Stir for ¼ of a minute and stir in tomatoes. Cook for about 3 minutes. Add bhindi, mix well, cover and cook on low heat for 8 to 10 minutes (turning them over once or twice).

The vegetable should not be too dry.

The first time I had this Bengali style preparation was in an Indian restaurant in London.

STUFFED BHINDI

Cooking time:
20 - 30 minutes

25 - 30 bhindi (large)
5 teaspoons of coriander powder
¼ teaspoon of chilli powder
¼ teaspoon of turmeric
¾ teaspoon of salt
¼ teaspoon of sugar
4 - 6 tablespoons lemon juice

Baghaar

4 tablespoons of oil
½ teaspoon of cumin seeds
½ teaspoon of asafoetida

Snip the top and bottom of the bhindi and make one insertion (lengthways) into each bhindi. Mix the spices, salt and lemon juice together. Stuff the bhindi evenly.

Heat oil in a wok. Add cumin seeds and asafoetida. When browned, add bhindi. Toss them gently around until they are well covered in oil. Cover and cook on low heat for 5 to 7 minutes (turning them over once or twice).

Remove the lid and leave roasting on a very low heat (turning from time to time) until crispy.

This North Indian style bhindi is a bit of a bother to prepare as you have to stuff each little bhindi with the masala but it's definitely worth the trouble.

CRISPY BHINDI (Rajasthani)

Cooking time:
20 - 30 minutes

¼ kg bhindi
½ teaspoon of coriander powder
¼ teaspoon of chilli powder
¼ teaspoon of turmeric
½ teaspoon of salt
¼ teaspoon of cumin powder
¼ teaspoon of asafoetida
1 teaspoon of dry oregano
4 tablespoons of gram flour

OIL FOR FRYING

Snip the top and bottom of the bhindi and slice them into very thin, long pieces.

Mix all the dry ingredients together.

Sprinkle the mixture onto the sliced bhindi and mix together gently making sure that all of the bhindi pieces are well coated with it.

Heat oil in a wok. When the oil is hot, loosely sprinkle the appropriate amount of bhindi mix into it and deep fry.

Repeat the process until all the mix is done. Serve hot.

This is another dish that is worth the effort. This was a very tasty surprise for me when I ate it in a restaurant in London. Its crispiness worked extremely well with dal, rice and other vegetables.

CABBAGE WITH POTATOES

Cooking time:
15 - 20 minutes

½ kg cabbage (chopped fine)
1 medium potato
(peeled and chopped into 8 pieces)
1 teaspoon of coriander powder
¼ teaspoon of crushed chillies
¼ teaspoon of turmeric
½ teaspoon of salt

Baghaar

2 tablespoons of oil
½ teaspoon of cumin seeds
½ teaspoon of asafoetida

Heat oil in a wok. Add cumin seeds and asafoetida. When browned, add potato pieces, cabbage and all the other ingredients. Stir well, cover and cook on a low heat for 7 to 10 minutes. Ensure that all water has evaporated.

This dish can be cooked with green peas.
Instead of the potatoes, add ¼ cup of peas.

This dish can be cooked with tomatoes.
In the final stage of cooking, instead of potato, add 1 medium tomato, chopped into 4 pieces.

This dish can be served dry or with some gravy.

Cabbage can produce surprisingly tasty results if it is cooked in its own juices. This one is from my naniji's kitchen. I like this best with rotis or parathas.

RED CABBAGE WITH POTATOES

Cooking time:
15 - 20 minutes

½ kg cabbage (chopped fine)
1 medium potato (peeled and chopped into 8 pieces)
1 teaspoon of coriander powder
¼ teaspoon of crushed chillies
¼ teaspoon of turmeric
½ teaspoon of salt

Baghaar

2 tablespoons of oil
½ teaspoon of fenugreek seeds
½ teaspoon of cumin seeds
½ teaspoon of asafoetida

Heat oil in a wok. Add fenugreek and, when they pop add cumin seeds and asafoetida. When browned add potatoes, cabbage and all other ingredients.

Stir well, cover and cook on a low heat for 7 to 10 minutes. Ensure that all water has evaporated.

We don't (or in my days, didn't) get red cabbage in India. In my early years in London, along with greens and other such vegetables, I learnt to make use of red cabbage to compensate for the lack of Indian vegetables. It is a bit strong in flavour but I like it cooked in this style.

KOFTA

Cooking time:
40 - 45 minutes

Kofta

¼ kg cabbage - red or green (grated)
1 cup of gram flour
¼ cup green coriander leaves (chopped)
OR 2 tablespoons of dry oregano
½ teaspoon of salt
1 green chilli (very finely chopped)

OIL TO FRY

Sauce

½ kg tomatoes (chopped very fine or squashed if tinned)
2 teaspoons of coriander powder
¼ teaspoon of crushed chillies
¼ teaspoon of turmeric
1 teaspoon of fennel powder
¾ teaspoon of salt
½ teaspoon of sugar
¼ cup green coriander leaves (chopped)
1 cup of water

Baghaar

6 tablespoons of oil
2 medium onions (chopped very fine)
½ teaspoon of cumin seeds
1 tablespoon of garlic (chopped fine)

Kofta: Mix all the ingredients for kofta with about 2 tablespoons of oil (the mixture consistency should be doughy therefore if soft add some more gram flour). Make about 12 rounded koftas with the mixture. Heat (medium to high) the rest of the oil in a wok and fry the koftas until golden brown.

Sauce: Heat 6 spoons of oil in a pan and add cumin seeds. When brown, add the onion and fry until nicely golden. Add garlic and all the other spices. Stir for a few seconds and add the tomatoes. Stir well, cover and cook on a low heat for 10 to 15 minutes (or until the liquid evaporates and oil shows).

Before serving, add water to the tomato sauce, bring it to boil and add the koftas. Reduce the heat and cook for 3 to 5 minutes. The koftas should be sitting in thick gravy, therefore add water if necessary.

Sprinkle with coriander and serve.

This dish can be made with courgettes instead of cabbage.

I love koftas with any kind of flat bread. It's a rich but very satisfying dish and evocative of the Persian influence on Indian Cusine.

CARROTS WITH LEMON

Cooking time:
15 - 20 minutes

½ kg carrots (round slices)
1 teaspoon of coriander powder
¼ teaspoon of crushed chillies
¼ teaspoon of turmeric
¾ teaspoon of salt
3 - 4 tablespoons of lemon juice
¼ cup green coriander leaves (chopped)

Baghaar

2 tablespoons of oil
½ teaspoon of cumin seeds
½ teaspoon of asafoetida

Heat oil in a wok. Add cumin seeds and asafoetida. When browned, add carrots and all the other ingredients (except lemon juice). Stir well, cover and cook on low heat for 5 to 7 minutes.

The vegetable should be dry. Sprinkle lemon juice, green coriander, mix and serve.

Athough I am not keen on carrots as a vegetable (because it is a bit on the sweet side), it is very nutritive and adds to the sweet and sour range.

CARROTS WITH DILL

Cooking time:
15 - 20 minutes

¼ kg carrots (round slices)
2 bunches of fresh dill
OR ½ cup of dry dill
1 teaspoon of coriander powder
¼ teaspoon of crushed chillies
¼ teaspoon of turmeric
½ teaspoon of salt

Baghaar

2 tablespoons of oil
½ teaspoon of cumin seeds
½ teaspoon of asafoetida

If using dry dill, soak it in ¾ cup of warm water.

Heat oil in a wok. Add cumin seeds and asafoetida. When browned, add carrots, dill and all the other ingredients.

Stir well, cover and cook on low heat for 5 to 7 minutes. The vegetable should be dry.

This dish can be made by substituting carrots with cauliflower.

My sister, Bandi, uses cauliflower instead of carrots.
Both versions are best complemented by rotis or parathas.

CARROTS WITH POTATOES

Cooking time:
15 - 20 minutes

less than ½ kg of carrots (cut into square pieces)
1 medium potato (chopped into 6 pieces)
1 teaspoon of coriander powder
¼ teaspoon of crushed chillies
¼ teaspoon of turmeric
¾ teaspoon of salt
½ cup of water
3 - 4 tablespoons of lemon juice
¼ cup green coriander leaves (chopped)

Baghaar

2 tablespoons of oil
½ teaspoon of cumin seeds
½ teaspoon of asafoetida

Heat oil in a wok. Add cumin seeds and asafoetida. When browned, add the vegetables and all other ingredients (except lemon juice).

Stir well, add the water, bring it to the boil, cover and cook on a low heat for 5 to 7 minutes.

The vegetable should have slight gravy. Sprinkle lemon juice, green coriander, mix and serve.

This dish can be made by substituting carrots with beetroots (chopped in chunky pieces).

My daughter Priya loves this dish, especially the beetroot version which she best enjoys when made by our friend Chandra.

CAULIFLOWER WITH CREAM AND ALMONDS

Cooking time:
20 - 25 minutes

1 medium cauliflower
(chopped into medium size pieces)
1 teaspoon of coriander powder
1 teaspoon of garam masala
pinch of crushed chillies
¾ teaspoon of salt
½ cup of thick cream
¼ cup of milk
2 good size cloves of garlic (finely chopped)
¼ cup green coriander leaves (chopped)

Baghaar

1½ tablespoons of butter
½ teaspoon of cumin seeds
12 split almonds (optional)
1 large onion (finely chopped)

Heat butter in a good size pan. Add cumin seeds and almonds. When browned, mix in the onions and fry gently until translucent.

Add coriander, garam masala and crushed chillies, toss for a few seconds. Add milk. Simmer for 2 to 3 minutes and add cauliflower, garlic and salt. Mix well and cover the pan.

Leave to simmer until cauliflower is tender (but not soft). Add the cream and simmer for 1 to 2 minutes. Before serving sprinkle with green coriander.

This is one of my favourite cauliflower dishes. A friend of the family once took me to a restaurant in London and on the menu there were a number of Kashmiri dishes. Never having tasted Kashmiri food, this was my chance. The only unusual vegetarian offering was cauliflower with cream so I had that and I just loved it. It has such delicate flavours and is just yummy, especially with nan.

CAULIFLOWER WITH POTATOES

Cooking time:
15 - 20 minutes

1 small cauliflower (chopped into medium size pieces)
2 medium potatoes (peeled and chopped into 4 pieces each)
1 teaspoon of coriander powder
¼ teaspoon of crushed chillies
¼ teaspoon of turmeric
¾ teaspoon of salt
1 tablespoon of ginger (chopped fine)
¼ cup green coriander leaves (chopped)

Baghaar

3 tablespoons of oil
½ teaspoon of cumin seeds
½ teaspoon of asafoetida

Heat oil in a wok. Add cumin seeds and asafoetida. When browned, add potatoes, cauliflower and all the other ingredients.

Stir well, cover and cook on low heat for 7 to 10 minutes.

Ensure that all the water has evaporated.

Sprinkle green coriander before serving.

This dish can be cooked with tomatoes:
Reduce potatoes to 1 and (once the potato is cooked) add 1 medium tomato, chopped into 4. It can be served dry or with some gravy.

CAULIFLOWER IN GARAM MASALA

Cooking time:
15 - 20 minutes

1 medium cauliflower (chopped into medium size pieces)
1 teaspoon of coriander powder
¼ teaspoon of crushed chillies
1 teaspoon of garam masala
½ teaspoon of salt
1 tablespoon of ginger (chopped fine)

Baghaar

4 tablespoons of oil
½ teaspoon of cumin seeds
½ teaspoon of asafoetida
2 whole green chillies (optional)

Heat oil in a wok. Add cumin seeds and asafoetida. When browned, add green chillies, cauliflower and all other ingredients (except salt).

Stir well cover and cook on low heat for 5 to 7 minutes until the cauliflower is tender.

Add salt and stir fry on a high heat until the vegetable is completely dry.

From grade six to eight of school, one of my best friends was a Bengali girl, Kumkum. We were what one would term bosom pals. Lots of sleepovers, sharing all the teenage secrets and so on. Her mother used to, like me, love cooking and feeding. She cooked fantastically well and this is one of her recipes. Sadly Kumkum was moved to a school nearer to her home. Did we cry! We continued meeting for a while and every time we met we wept copiously. But as life goes, in time we both drifted apart and into new friend circles. Needless to say I missed her mum's cooking as much as I missed Kumkum .

CAULIFLOWER WITH POTATOES, TOMATOES AND ONIONS

Cooking time:
20 - 25 minutes

1 small cauliflower (chopped into medium size pieces)
1 medium potato (peeled and chopped into 4 to 6 pieces)
2 medium tomatoes (chopped into 4 pieces each)
2 teaspoons of coriander powder
¼ teaspoon of crushed chillies
¼ teaspoon of turmeric powder
¾ teaspoon of salt
1 tablespoon of ginger (chopped)
¼ cup green coriander leaves (chopped)

Baghaar

6 tablespoons of oil
½ teaspoon of cumin seeds
1 large onion (chopped lengthwise)

Heat oil in a pan. Add cumin seeds. As soon as they brown, add the onions and fry until nicely browned.

Add ginger and all the other spices. Stir for ¼ of a minute and stir in potatoes. Cook for about 3 minutes.

Add cauliflower, mix well and cover the pan. Cook on gentle heat for 5 to 7 minutes. Stir in tomatoes and cook for another 5 minutes.

Before serving garnish with coriander.

This is regular Punjabi fare. It goes well with thick rotis.

CAULIFLOWER WITH DESICCATED COCONUT (Parsi)

Cooking time:
20 - 25 minutes

1 medium cauliflower (chopped into medium size pieces)
1 cup of desiccated coconut or ½ cup of coconut cream
1 teaspoon of coriander powder
¼ teaspoon of chilli powder
¾ teaspoon of salt
1 teaspoon of garlic (finely chopped)
6 curry leaves
1 cup of milk
¼ cup green coriander leaves (chopped)

Baghaar

3 tablespoons of oil
½ teaspoon of mustard seeds
1 large onion (finely chopped)

Heat oil in a pan. Add mustard seeds. As soon they pop, add the onions and fry until nicely browned.

Add curry leaves, garlic, coconut and all the other spices. Stir for ¼ of a minute, add milk and cook for a minute on low heat.

Add cauliflower and simmer for about 7 to 10 minutes on low heat.

Before serving garnish with coriander.

Katie and her mum will be proud of me to see how well I have mastered this dish.

CAULIFLOWER PAKORAS IN TANDOORI SAUCE

Cooking time:
40 - 45 minutes

12 - 16 pieces of cauliflower pakoras (see page 48)
1 cup of yoghurt
1 cup of water
½ teaspoon of plain flour
3 teaspoons of tandoori masala
½ teaspoon of salt
½ cup green coriander leaves (chopped)

Baghaar

2 tablespoons of oil
½ teaspoon of cumin seeds
1 teaspoon of garlic (chopped fine)

Mix yoghurt, water, flour, salt and tandoori masala together.

Heat oil in a pan. Add cumin seeds and garlic. When browned, stir in yoghurt, mix and simmer on a low heat for 5 minutes.

Just before serving, toss the pakoras in the tandoori sauce, heat quickly, sprinkle coriander and serve.

Food-wise Goa is a delight for fish eaters and quite a trial for vegetarians. The majority of restaurants and cafes offer a very mundane fare to non-fish/meat eaters. Also, generally it is difficult to find places offering the food of the region. On a holiday there some years ago, while Gordon indulged himself night after night to yet another fish delight, I sat eating mostly boiled rice and cabbage. However, one evening I found this dish on the menu and forgave Goa for all its food-limitations. This is, by its ingredients, a North Indian concoction but eating it on a Goa beach, with the waves gently lapping only a few feet away added even more pleasure to this tangy delight.

CAULIFLOWER LEAVES WITH POTATOES

Cooking time:
15 - 20 minutes

leaves of 1 cauliflower (chopped fine)
1 medium potato (peeled and chopped into 8 pieces)
1 teaspoon of coriander powder
¼ teaspoon of crushed chillies
¼ teaspoon of turmeric
1 teaspoon amchoor
½ teaspoon of salt

Baghaar

2 tablespoons of oil
½ teaspoon of cumin seeds
½ teaspoon of asafoetida

Heat oil in a wok. Add cumin seeds and asafoetida. When browned, add potato pieces, leaves and all the other ingredients (except amchoor).

Stir well, cover and cook on a low heat for 7 to 10 minutes, add amchoor and cook further till vegetable is dry.

India has an age old tradition of maximising on every bit of any object – be it cauliflower leaves or rubber tyres - 'waste not want not' - a recycling policy at its best. In North India the leaves of cauliflower invariably get used up as an extra vegetable - making a very tasty and nutritional dish indeed. And some of us, in fact, like it very much with our parathas. The cauliflowers in UK, in the early 70s, had their leaves trimmed off prior to being sold. A Punjabi friend of mine in London, who loved this dish to no end, resorted to going behind the market stalls and, to the amazement of the stall holders, gathering up the thrown leaves. The stall holders probably thought of her as a 'poverty striken Indian.' I also use up these leaves in soups or other such dishes.

Courgettes, Marrow, Tori and Lauki

- ◆ Courgettes, Marrow, Tori and Lauki are interchangeable.

- ◆ Courgettes do not need peeling.

- ◆ Marrow needs peeling only if the skin is hard.

- ◆ Tori & Lauki need scraping/peeling depending on the softness/hardness of the skin.

- ◆ Tori and Lauki are one of the easiest vegetables to digest and therefore often given, cooked with a touch of spice, to recuperating patients.

COURGETTES, MARROW, TORI OR LAUKI WITH LEMON

Cooking time:
15 - 20 minutes

½ kg courgettes, marrow, tori or lauki
(if courgettes or tori, chopped into round, 1cm pieces)
(if marrow or lauki, chopped into 2cm cubes)
¾ teaspoon of coriander powder
¼ teaspoon of crushed chillies
¼ teaspoon of turmeric
¾ teaspoon of salt
¼ teaspoon of sugar
3 - 4 tablespoons of lemon juice

Baghaar

½ tablespoon of butter/ghee
¼ teaspoon of cumin seeds
¼ teaspoon of asafoetida

Heat oil in a wok. Add cumin seeds and asafoetida. When browned, add the vegetable and all the other ingredients (except lemon juice and sugar).

Stir well, cover and cook on a low heat for 5 to 7 minutes. The vegetable will have a slight gravy.

Add lemon juice and sugar and cook for a minute or two.

This dish can be cooked with yoghurt:
In the last step instead of lemon juice mix in ¼ cup of yoghurt.

This is a delicate, aromatic dish from my naniji's kitchen

COURGETTES OR MARROW WITH POTATOES AND GARLIC

Cooking time:
15 - 20 minutes

**Under ½ kg of courgettes or marrow
(chopped into 2cm size pieces)
1 medium potato (chopped into 6 pieces)
1 teaspoon of coriander powder
¼ teaspoon of crushed chillies
¼ teaspoon of turmeric powder
1 teaspoon of garam masala
¾ teaspoon of salt**

Baghaar

**4 tablespoons of oil
½ teaspoon of cumin seeds
1 tablespoon of garlic (chopped fine)**

Heat oil in a pan. Add cumin seeds. As soon as they brown, add the garlic and all the other spices. Mix in the potato pieces and toss the mixture around for 2 to 3 minutes.

Stir in the vegetable. Mix well and cover the pan. Cook on gentle heat for 5 to 7 minutes. The dish should have some gravy (if it is too dry add a few spoons of water).

As a teenager, every summer I, with my family, travelled to Baripada, my birth place. We took a train from Mumbai to Kolkata and from there had to change once again to reach Baripada. After 36 hours on the train, at Kolkata's Howra station, we showered, changed and had lunch in the station restaurant before boarding our connecting train. It was there that I first tried this dish with rice and dal, liked it very much and immediately stored it in my brain computer to be retrieved years later in London, when only a few vegetables were available each season and everyone of them had to be cooked in more and more different ways to give a notion of variety.

COURGETTES OR MARROW WITH POTATOES AND TANDOORI MASALA

Cooking time:
15 - 20 minutes

**Under ½ kg of courgettes or marrow
(chopped into medium size pieces)
1 medium potato (chopped into 6 pieces)
3 teaspoons of tandoori masala
½ teaspoon of salt
¼ cup green coriander leaves (chopped)**

Baghaar

**4 tablespoons of oil
½ teaspoon of cumin seeds
1 tablespoon of garlic (chopped fine)**

Heat oil in a pan. Add cumin seeds. As soon as they brown, add the garlic and potatoes and toss around for 2 to 3 minutes.

Add tandoori masala and stir in the vegetable. Mix well and cover the pan. Cook on a gentle heat for 5 to 7 minutes.

Before serving, sprinkle the coriander.

This dish can also be cooked with yoghurt or cream: Add ¼ cup of either in the final stage and gently simmer for another 2 to 3 minutes.

Being creative and trying to expand my repertoire I experimented a bit and came up with this very quick and delicious recipe.

COURGETTES OR MARROW WITH TOMATOES

Cooking time:
15 - 20 minutes

½ kg of courgettes/marrow
(chopped into medium size pieces)
2 medium tomatoes (chopped into medium size pieces)
1 teaspoon of coriander powder
¼ teaspoon of cumin powder
¼ teaspoon of chilli powder
¼ teaspoon of turmeric
¾ teaspoon of salt
¼ teaspoon of sugar
½ cup green coriander leaves (chopped)

Baghaar

4 tablespoons of oil
1 teaspoon of cumin seeds
½ teaspoon of asafoetida

Heat oil in a pan. Add cumin seeds and when they pop add asafoetida. When browned, add the vegetable and all the other spices. Stir well, cover and cook on low heat for 5 to 7 minutes turning it around once or twice.

Add the tomatoes and cook for another 5 to 7 minutes. The dish should be on the wet side.

Before serving, garnish with coriander.

COURGETTES, MARROW, TORI OR LAUKI WITH COCONUT (South Indian)

Cooking time:
15 - 20 minutes

½ kg of courgettes/marrow/tori/lauki
(chopped into 2cm size pieces)
2 tablespoons of desiccated coconut
OR coconut cream
1 teaspoon of coriander powder
¼ teaspoon of chilli powder
½ teaspoon of salt
6 curry leaves
¼ cup green coriander leaves (chopped)

Baghaar

2 tablespoons of oil
½ teaspoon of mustard seeds
1 tablespoon of urad dal
1 large onion (finely chopped)

Heat oil in a pan. Add mustard seeds. As soon as they pop, add the dal. When brown, add the onion and fry until translucent. Add curry leaves, coconut and all the other spices. Stir for half a minute.

Add the vegetable, cover pan and simmer for about 5 to 7 minutes on low heat. Before serving garnish with coriander.

This dish can also be cooked with yoghurt.
In the final step, mix in ¼ cup of yoghurt and extra salt.

Mahabalipuram, near Chenai, is famous for its Sun temple. But me being a foody will always remember Mahabalipuram for lunching al fresco on the beach, eating lauki cooked this way, with sambhar, rice and other tit-bits. It was a most blissful lunch with the sea breeze bringing the temperature down and the sound of waves crashing.

GREEN BANANA (Dry)

Cooking time:
15 - 20 minutes

½ kg of raw banana
(boiled whole in skin and chopped into 2cm size round slices)
1 teaspoon of coriander powder
¼ teaspoon of crushed chillies
¼ teaspoon of turmeric
½ teaspoon of salt

Baghaar

2 tablespoons of oil
½ teaspoon of cumin seeds
½ teaspoon of asafoetida

Heat oil in a wok. Add cumin seeds and asafoetida. When browned, add banana and all the other ingredients. Stir well and cook on low heat for 5 to 7 minutes.

Before serving, cook the banana on medium heat until slightly crispy.

This dish works really well with parathas.

GREEN BANANA WITH LEMON

Cooking time:
15-20 minutes

½ kg raw banana
(boiled whole in skin and chopped into 2cm round slices)
1 teaspoon of coriander powder
¼ teaspoon of crushed chillies
¼ teaspoon of turmeric
¾ teaspoon of salt
1 cup of water
3 - 4 tablespoons of lemon juice

Baghaar

2 tablespoons of oil
½ teaspoon of ajwain seeds
½ teaspoon of asafoetida

Heat oil in a pan. Add ajwain seeds and asafoetida. When browned, add banana and all the other ingredients (except lemon juice).

Stir well, cover and cook on low heat for a minute. Add water, bring to boil and cook for a further 5 to 7 minutes on a low heat.

Sprinkle lemon juice, mix and cook for a minute. The vegetable should have some gravy.

This ones goes even better with parathas.

GREEN BANANA WITH COCONUT (South Indian)

Cooking time:
20 - 25 minutes

½ kg raw banana
(boiled whole in skin and chopped into 2cm cubes)
½ cup of desiccated coconut
½ cup of yoghurt
½ cup of water
1 teaspoon of coriander powder
¼ teaspoon of chilli powder
¾ teaspoon of salt
¼ cup green coriander leaves (chopped)

Baghaar

2 tablespoons of oil
½ teaspoon of mustard seeds
6 curry leaves
1 large onion (finely chopped)

Heat oil in a pan. Add mustard seeds. As soon as they pop, add onions and fry until translucent. Add curry leaves coconut, yogurt and all the other spices. Stir for ¼ of a minute.

Add the vegetable, stir for a minute and add the water. Cover the pan and simmer for about 5 to 7 minutes on a low heat.

Before serving, garnish with coriander.

This dish can be made with a mixture of vegetables such as banana, courgette, peppers, etc.

This is absolutely delicious with rice.

GREEN BEANS WITH POTATOES

Cooking time:
15 - 20 minutes

½ kg green beans
(chopped into 2cm pieces)
1 medium potato - optional
(peeled and chopped into 8 pieces)
1 teaspoon of coriander powder
¼ teaspoon of crushed chillies
¼ teaspoon of turmeric
½ teaspoon of salt
3 - 4 tablespoons of lemon juice

Baghaar

2 tablespoons of oil
½ teaspoon of cumin seeds
½ teaspoon of asafoetida

Green beans come in many varieties and can be cooked in as many ways. For the recipes here you can use whichever is available or your favourite kind.

Heat oil in a wok. Add cumin seeds and asafoetida. When browned, add potatoes, beans and all the other ingredients (except lemon juice).

Stir well, cover and cook on low heat for 5 to 7 minutes. Toss the mixture on high heat for a minute or two or until all the water has evaporated. Sprinkle lemon juice, toss for another minute on heat and serve.

I loved beans cooked this way by my grandmother. The delicacy of their shape and flavour aptly matched these particular beans' name, Rambha Phali. In Hindu mythology, Rambha was considered as one of the four most beautiful and delicate Apsaras – Urvashi, Menaka and Tilottama being the other three. Apsaras were supposed to be strikingly beautiful and talented women who resided in heaven and charmed the gods there with their exquisiteness and entertained them with their arts. Apsaras were often sent to earth by the gods to distract sages from their deep meditation - meditation that would help the sages accumulate powers that might threaten the gods.

GREEN BEANS WITH DESICCATED COCONUT (Parsi)

Cooking time:
20 - 25 minutes

½ kg green beans
(chopped into 2cm pieces)
1 cup of desiccated coconut
OR ½ cup of coconut cream
2 teaspoons of coriander powder
¼ teaspoon of chilli powder
1 teaspoon of garlic (finely chopped)
¾ teaspoon of salt
1 cup of milk
¼ cup green coriander leaves (chopped)

Baghaar

4 tablespoons of oil
½ teaspoon of mustard seeds
6 curry leaves
1 large onion (finely chopped)

Heat oil in a pan. Add mustard seeds. As soon as they pop, add the onions and fry until nicely browned. Add curry leaves, garlic, coconut and all other spices. Stir for a few seconds, add milk and cook for a few minutes on low heat.

Add beans, cover the pan and cook for about 5 to 7 minutes on a low heat. Before serving, garnish with coriander.

This dish can also be cooked with tomatoes. Replace the milk with 2 medium size tomatoes, sliced small.

Years ago I watched my friend Katie slice runner beans by hand diagonally - thin and long and totally uniform (it was just mesmerising) - and produce this scrumptious dish.

GREEN BEANS WITH POTATOES, TOMATOES AND ONIONS

Cooking time:
20 - 25 minutes

less than ½ kg green beans
(chopped into 2cm pieces)
1 medium potato
(peeled and chopped into 8 long pieces)
2 medium tomatoes
(chopped into 4 pieces each)
1 teaspoon of coriander powder
¼ teaspoon of crushed chillies
¼ teaspoon of turmeric powder
1 teaspoon of salt
½ teaspoon of garam masala
1 teaspoon of garlic (chopped)
¼ cup green coriander leaves

Baghaar

4 tablespoons of oil
½ teaspoon of cumin seeds
1 large onion (chopped lengthwise)

Heat oil in a pan. Add cumin seeds, as soon as they brown, add the onions and fry until nicely browned. Add garlic and all other spices. Stir for 15 seconds or so and stir in the potato. Cook for about 3 minutes.

Add beans, mix well and cover the pan. Cook on gentle heat for 5 to 7 minutes, stir in tomatoes and cook for another 5 minutes. Before serving, sprinkle the garam masala and the coriander.

Try this dish with couscous or bulgar wheat cooked
with nuts and herbs – absolutely perfect.

GREEN BEANS WITH URAD DAL (South Indian)

Cooking time:
15 - 20 minutes

½ kg beans (chopped very small)
1 tablespoon of urad dal
2 tablespoons of desiccated coconut
1 teaspoon of coriander powder
¼ teaspoon of chilli powder
½ teaspoon of salt
¼ cup green coriander leaves (chopped)

Baghaar

4 tablespoons of oil
½ teaspoon of mustard seeds
6 curry leaves
1 large onion (finely chopped)

Heat oil in a pan. Add mustard seeds, as soon as they pop, add the onions and fry until translucent. Add the beans and all the other ingredients, cover the pot and cook for 3 to 5 minutes on a low heat.

Before serving, mix in the coconut, cook for another 3 - 4 minutes and garnish with fresh coriander.

Some years ago Gordon, my partner, and I travelled around Kerala in South India, the greenest place I have ever been to. We ended our travels with a trip on the backwaters, drifting in a rice-boat, converted into a floating holiday home, for three days on the calm, tranquil waters. All our meals and snacks were prepared on the boat with the fresh supplies picked up en-route. For Gordon, the cook prepared various fish dishes and for me all vegetarian fare. I used to watch him grind to paste various blends of spices, or roast roughly ground coriander, chilli, etc. Whatever he dished out at the end was absolutely delicious – and the tastes and flavours were further enhanced by the greenery we were floating through, the gentle lapping of the water and the world gliding by.

Karela

Karela, known as bitter gourd in English, is a truly bitter vegetable. Added to this is its peculiar appearance – almost crocodile like shape and dark to pale green rough skin - making it not much liked by many. But of course for me its bitterness is what makes it so special, affording it a unique taste. But it's the vegetable's preventative and curative qualities that make it really significant.

Karela is said to stimulate digestion, is good for the liver and has been traditionally used in Ayurveda to regulate blood sugar levels. Its extract can now be bought in capsule form. Most people try to rid it of its bitterness mainly by scraping the skin. Some also slit the scraped karela, salt it inside-out and leave it for a few hours to rid it of its juices. They further squeeze the vegetable before cooking. To me, all this is a travesty as in the process one loses all the valuable properties of the vegetable.

For the recipes here I cook the vegetable, skin and all. But if you do prefer to reduce its bitterness then by all means scrape the skin.

CRISPY KARELA

Cooking time:
15 - 20 minutes

½ kg of karela (chopped into thin round pieces)
½ teaspoon of coriander powder
¼ teaspoon of crushed chillies
¼ teaspoon of turmeric
½ teaspoon of salt

Baghaar

3 tablespoons of oil
½ teaspoon of cumin seeds
½ teaspoon of asafoetida

Heat oil in a wok. Add cumin seeds and asafoetida. When browned, add karela and all other ingredients (except salt).

Stir well and cook on a low heat for 5 to 7 minutes and add salt. Before serving, cook karela on a low heat until crispy.

According to Ayurveda, all food can be categorized into six key tastes – sweet, sour, bitter, pungent, astringent and salty – all essential not only for the proper functioning of our bodies but also for inclusive taste. Ayurvedic principles of food suggest that as far as possible we need to include all the six tastes or as many as possible, for the creation of a perfectly tasteful meal. In South India, to complete the six tastes, the main meal is often served with chutneys made with astringent fruits and a small amount of crispy karela.

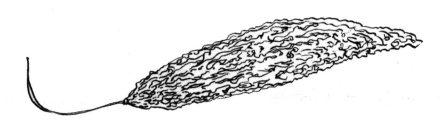

KARELA WITH LEMON

Cooking time:
15 - 20 minutes

½ kg of karela (chopped into thin round pieces)
1 teaspoon of coriander powder
¼ teaspoon of crushed chillies
¼ teaspoon of turmeric
¾ teaspoon of salt
3 - 4 tablespoons of lemon juice

Baghaar

2 tablespoons of oil
½ teaspoon of cumin seeds
½ teaspoon of asafoetida

Heat oil in a wok. Add cumin seeds and asafoetida. When browned, add karela and all the other ingredients (except lemon juice). Stir well, cover and cook on a low heat for 5 to 7 minutes.

The vegetable should be dry but not crispy. Sprinkle the lemon juice, mix and serve.

Karela is one of the vegetables I love and have no problem with it in regards to its bitterness. In fact as a child, in my naniji's home, I used to ask my naniji to extract the juice from the scraped karela skin and drink it as a dare. Now, that was bitter and more, but I am sure it did me a lot of good. This is from my naniji's kitchen and yes, as you may have guessed, she used to scrape the skin.

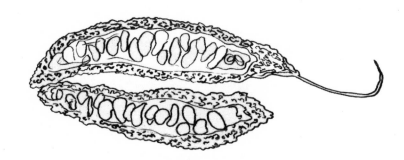

KARELA WITH TOMATOES

Cooking time:
15 - 20 minutes

**Under ½ kg of karela
(chopped into thick round pieces)
2 medium tomatoes (chopped into small slices)
1 teaspoon of coriander powder
¼ teaspoon of crushed chillies
¼ teaspoon of turmeric
¾ teaspoon of salt
½ teaspoon of ginger (paste)
½ teaspoon of garlic (paste)**

Baghaar

**3 tablespoons of oil
½ teaspoon of cumin seeds
1 medium onion (chopped small)**

Heat oil in a pan. Add cumin seeds. As soon as they brown, add the onions and fry until nicely browned.

Add ginger, garlic and all the other spices. Stir for ¼ of a minute and stir in the tomatoes. Cook for about 3 minutes.

Add karela, mix well, cover and cook on a low heat for 8 to 10 minutes (turning them over once or twice). The vegetable should not be too dry.

STUFFED KARELA (North Indian)

Cooking time:
15 - 20 minutes

6 small (8 to 10 cm long) karela (the skin scraped)
4 teaspoons of coriander powder
¼ teaspoon of chilli powder
¼ teaspoon of turmeric
¾ teaspoon of salt
¼ teaspoon of sugar
3 - 4 tablespoons of lemon juice

Baghaar

2 tablespoons of oil
½ teaspoon of cumin seeds
½ teaspoon of asafoetida

Carefully make one incision (lengthways) into each karela so as not to cut them apart at the top or the bottom. Mix the spices, salt and lemon juice together. Divide the mixture roughly into six portions and stuff the karela.

Heat oil in a wok. Add cumin seeds and asafoetida. When browned, add the karela. Toss them around until they are well covered in oil. Cover and cook on low heat for 5 to 7 minutes (turning them over once or twice).

Remove the lid and leave roasting on a very low heat (and turning them from time to time) until the skin turns nice and crispy.

Naniji often used to make this for the evening meal. Once the baghaar was done she used to leave them cooking on the lowest possible heat for hours, turning them around now and again. They slow cooked into perfect crispiness outside while still succulent inside. I was known for pinching one or two of these well before the meal. I love this karela with parathas.

Paneer

Paneer (cheese), although placed in the vegetable category (by me), is by no means a vegetable. It is a milk product full of protein, calcium and some fat. It is also lighter than milk to digest and thus given particularly to people who need proteins, but have digestion problems. I have included it in this section a) because it is often mixed with a vegetable and b) because it is used as an acompaniment to dal etc.

Paneer is one of the most versatile milk products and can be turned into sweet or savoury dishes. It is mainly used in Bengal (mostly for sweets) and Punjab (mostly for savoury dishes) but spreading gradually to other parts of India - in the south I have eaten dosas (rice and lentil pancakes) sprinkled with grated paneer.

It is often combined with other vegetables to give it an extra flavour and taste. Many supermarkets now stock it in their cheese section but it can also be bought from any South Asian grocery store. Of course paneer can also be made at home (see pg 43 for recipe). In the recipes here I have used ready-made paneer as a shortcut. As paneer itself is quite rich I avoid using ingredients such as nuts with it for they would make the dish even heavier. The only exception to this is cream – the combination of paneer and cream make an absolute treat.

PANEER WITH CREAM

Cooking time:
30 minutes

½ kg of paneer (chopped into 2cm cubes)
½ teaspoon of coriander powder
½ teaspoon of garam masala
¼ teaspoon of crushed chillies
½ teaspoon of salt
½ cup of thick cream
¼ cup of milk
1 tablespoon of garlic (finely chopped)
½ cup green coriander leaves (chopped)
oil for frying

Baghaar

4 tablespoons of oil
½ teaspoon of cumin seeds
10 - 12 split almonds (optional)
1 large onion (finely chopped)

Heat butter/oil in a good size pan. Add cumin seeds. When browned mix in the onions and fry gently until translucent.

Stir in the almonds, coriander, garam masala and crushed chillies. Add milk. Simmer for a minute and add paneer, garlic and salt. Mix well and cover the pan. Leave to cook on very low heat for 5 to 7 minutes. Add the cream and simmer for 1 minute.

Before serving, sprinkle the green coriander.

Once on a trip to India I met up with a few friends for a meal in a five star restaurant (a bit unusual for us). All the food we ordered was just scrumptious. But morsels of paneer in cream with crunchy nan, all accompanied by a crisp white wine were truly heavenly.

PANEER WITH TANDOORI MASALA

Cooking time:
15 - 20 minutes

½ kg of paneer (chopped into 2cm cubes)
4 teaspoons of tandoori masala
¾ teaspoon of salt
1 tablespoon of garlic (paste)
3 - 4 tablespoons of lemon juice
2 cups of water
½ cup of single cream (optional)
½ cup of green coriander leaves (chopped)

Baghaar

2 tablespoons of oil
½ teaspoon of cumin seeds

Heat oil in a wok and add the cumin seeds. As soon as they brown, stir in tandoori masala and garlic.

Mix in the paneer pieces and toss the paneer around for a minute. Add water, salt and lemon juice. Bring to the boil and simmer for a minute and turn the heat off.

Leave the mixture to marinate for 4 to 6 hours.

Before serving cook the mixture on low to medium heat until all the liquid has evaporated. Transfer to a serving dish, pour the cream (OPTIONAL) but do NOT MIX.

Sprinkle the green coriander.

This is one of my most innovative creations. Its tanginess, combined with the gritty sharp taste of masala and the red colour makes it a temptingly special dish.

PANEER WITH TOMATOES (Dry)

Cooking time:
25 minutes

Approximately 350 grams of paneer
(chopped into 1cm wide and 5 to 6cm length pieces)
2 medium tomatoes (chopped lengthways- 12 pieces)
1½ teaspoons of coriander powder
¼ teaspoon of crushed chillies
¾ teaspoon of salt
1 cup of green coriander leaves (chopped)

Baghaar

4 tablespoons of oil
1 teaspoon of cumin seeds
1 large onion (chopped lengthways)

Heat oil in a good size frying pan. Add cumin seeds. When browned, mix in the onions and fry gently until translucent.

Add coriander, crushed chillies, salt and paneer. Mix well and cook on low heat for 5 to 6 minutes (tossing it around once or twice).

Before serving, add tomatoes and green coriander. Stir for a minute or two and serve.

My older sister Manju was not a keen cook, especially before marriage. My brother-in-law on the other hand not only liked his food but was also a very good cook. In time Manju learnt to produce extremely tasty dishes and was proud of it. I learnt this mildly sweet succulent dish from her.

PANEER IN TOMATO GRAVY

Cooking time:
35 minutes

Approximately 350 grams of paneer
(chopped into 2cm cubes)
2 large tomatoes
(chopped small or 400g tinned tomatoes, squashed)
1½ teaspoons of coriander powder
¼ teaspoon of crushed chillies
1 teaspoon of fennel powder
¼ teaspoon of turmuric
¾ teaspoon of salt
½ cup of water
½ cup of green coriander leaves (chopped)

OIL FOR FRYING

Baghaar

6 tablespoons of oil
½ teaspoon of cumin seeds
1 tablespoon of garlic (chopped fine)
1 large onion (finely chopped)

Heat oil in a wok and fry the paneer pieces until golden brown (alternatively, they can be brushed with oil and grilled or sautéd).

Heat 6 spoons of oil in a good size frying pan. Add cumin seeds. When browned mix in the onions and fry until brown. Mix in garlic and all other spices.

Add tomatoes. Mix well and cook on high heat until the liquid has evaporated. Add paneer and cook for 5 to 6 minutes. Before serving add ½ cup of water and bring to boil. Sprinkle green coriander and serve.

I find this dish cooks better with tinned tomatoes

This is a favourite with most of my family, especially my grandson, Gethin, my son and his ex-girlfriend (for whom I still cook this from time to time). It is tangy, yet with a touch of sweetness and hits your palate with a mixture of flavours. Delicious with most flat breads.

PANEER WITH PEAS

Cooking time:
30 minutes

¼ kg of paneer (chopped into 2cm cubes)
1 cup of peas
1 large tomato (chopped small)
OR 1 tablespoon of tomato puree
1½ teaspoons of coriander powder
¼ teaspoon of turmeric powder
1 tablespoon of garlic (chopped fine)
¼ teaspoon of crushed chillies
¾ teaspoon of salt
¼ cup green coriander leaves (chopped)
1 cup of water

OIL FOR FRYING

Baghaar

4 tablespoons of oil
¼ teaspoon of cumin seeds
1 large onion (finely chopped)

Heat oil in a wok and fry the paneer pieces until golden brown (alternatively they can be brushed with oil and grilled or sautéd).

Heat oil in a good size frying pan, add cumin seeds. When browned, mix in the onions and fry until brown. Mix in the garlic and all the other spices and stir for a few seconds.

Add tomatoes and cook until the liquid has evaporated (with puree, the cooking time will be less). Mix in the paneer and peas, cover and cook on low heat for 3 to 4 minutes. Add water and cook for a further 5 to 7 minutes (tossing it around once or twice). Ensure that the vegetable is not dry. Before serving add coriander.

**This dish can be cooked without onions and garlic:
At the baghaar stage, with cumin seeds, add ½ teaspoon of asafoetida and leave out the onions and garlic altogether.**

This and paneer with spinach are standard dishes found on most Indian restaurant menus in the UK and in India.

PANEER WITH PEAS (2)

Cooking time:
30 minutes

¼ kg of paneer (crumbled up)
1 cup of peas
1 cup of sour yoghurt
1 tablespoon of garlic (finely chopped)
1 teaspoon of coriander powder
1 teaspoon of paprika
1 teaspoon of garam masala
¼ teaspoon of turmeric powder
¼ teaspoon of crushed chillies
¾ teaspoon of salt
¼ cup of green coriander leaves (chopped)

Baghaar

6 tablespoons of oil
½ teaspoon of cumin seeds
1 large onion (finely chopped)

Heat the oil in a good size frying pan. Add cumin seeds. When browned, mix in the onions and fry until brown. Add the paneer and cook on medium heat for 3 to 4 minutes.

Mix in the garlic and all the other spices. Fry for a minute and stir in the yoghurt. Add the peas. Mix well, cover and cook on low heat for 7 to 10 minutes (tossing it around once or twice).

Ensure that the vegetable is not too dry (add few spoons of water if necessary). Before serving add green coriander.

This recipe goes back to the days in London when I had to be at my creative best with a limited number of vegetables available at any given time. The family just loved it with rotis.

PEAS WITH POTATOES AND ONIONS

Cooking time:
30 minutes

2 cups of shelled peas
1 medium potato (peeled and chopped into 6 pieces)
2 teaspoons of coriander powder
¼ teaspoon of crushed chillies
¼ teaspoon of turmeric powder
½ teaspoon of salt
1 teaspoon of garlic (crushed)
1 teaspoon of ginger (crushed)
½ cup of water
½ teaspoon of garam masala

Baghaar

8 tablespoons of oil
½ teaspoon of cumin seeds
1 large onion (finely chopped)

Heat oil in a pan. Add cumin seeds. As soon as they brown add the onions and fry till nicely browned. Add garlic, ginger and all the other spices, except garam masala. Stir for a few seconds and stir in potato pieces. Cook for about 3 to 4 minutes.

Add peas, mix well, add water and cover the pan. Cook on gentle heat for 7 to 10 minutes. Ensure that the vegetable is not too dry. Add a spoon or two of water if necessary. Before serving, sprinkle with garam masala.

This dish can also be cooked with tomatoes:
After the potatoes have been cooked for 3 to 4 minutes, add 1 medium size fresh tomato (chopped fine) or 1 tablespoon of tomato puree and cook till liquid has evaporated. Also add extra salt.

I find frozen peas a bit too sweet – fresh ones are perfect for this dish.

STUFFED PEPPERS (North Indian)

Cooking time:
15 - 20 minutes

6 small (6 to 7 cm long) peppers
4 teaspoons of coriander powder
¼ teaspoon of chilli powder
¼ teaspoon of turmeric
¾ teaspoon of salt
¼ teaspoon of sugar
3 - 4 tablespoons of lemon juice

Baghaar

2 tablespoons of oil
½ teaspoon of cumin seeds
½ teaspoon of asafoetida

Make one long incision in each pepper carefully so as not to cut them apart.

Mix the spices, salt and lemon juice together. Divide the mixture roughly into 6 portions and stuff the peppers.

Heat oil in a wok. Add cumin seeds and asafoetida. When browned, add the peppers. Toss them around till they are well covered in oil. Cover and cook on a low heat for 5 to 7 minutes (turning them over once or twice).

Before serving, cook on a high heat for a few minutes.

This is a basic, simple dish that goes equally well with bread or rice.

STUFFED PEPPERS WITH GRAM FLOUR (Gujarati)

Cooking time:
15 - 20 minutes

6 small (6 to 7 cm long) peppers
4 tablespoons of gram flour
1 teaspoon of coriander powder
¼ teaspoon of chilli powder
¼ teaspoon of turmeric
¾ teaspoon of salt
½ teaspoon of sugar
3 - 4 tablespoons of lemon juice
3 - 4 tablespoons of water
2 tablespoons of oil

Baghaar

2 tablespoons of oil
½ teaspoon of asafoetida
½ teaspoon of mustard seeds

Make 1 long incision into each pepper carefully so as not to cut them apart.

Mix the gram flour, spices, salt, sugar, and lemon juice together. Add 2 tablespoons of oil to this and enough water to mix it into a thick paste. Divide the mixture roughly into 6 portions and stuff the peppers.

Heat oil in a wok. Add mustard seeds and when they pop add asafoetida. When browned, add the peppers. Toss them around till they are well covered in oil. Cover and cook on low heat for 8 to 12 minutes (turning them over once or twice).

Before serving, cook on a high heat for a few minutes.

I learned this in London from my Gujarati family.

STUFFED PEPPERS WITH MASHED POTATOES

Cooking time:
15 - 20 minutes

6 small (6 to 7 cm long) peppers
1 large potato (boiled and mashed)
1 teaspoon of garlic (paste)
½ cup green coriander leaves (chopped)
1 teaspoon of coriander powder
¼ teaspoon of chilli powder
¾ teaspoon of salt
¼ teaspoon of sugar
5 - 6 tablespoons of lemon juice
1 tablespoon of oil

Baghaar

2 tablespoons of oil
½ teaspoon of cumin seeds
½ teaspoon of asafoetida

Make 1 long incision in each pepper carefully so as not to cut them apart.

Mix the mashed potato, coriander, spices, salt, sugar, one tablespoonful of oil and lemon juice together. Divide the mixture roughly into 6 portions and stuff the peppers.

Heat oil in a wok. Add cumin seeds and asafoetida. When browned, add the peppers. Toss them around till they are well covered in oil, cover and cook on low heat for 8 to 12 minutes (turning them over once or twice).

Before serving, cook on a high heat for a few minutes.

This is another of my inspirations that turned out delectably satisfying.

PEPPERS WITH POTATOES

Cooking time:
30 minutes

½ kg of peppers - red or green or mixture
(chopped into 3cm pieces)
1 large potato (chopped into 8 pieces)
1 teaspoon of coriander powder
1 teaspoon of paprika
1 teaspoons of garlic (chopped fine)
¼ teaspoon of crushed chillies
¼ teaspoon of turmeric powder
¾ teaspoon of salt

Baghaar

8 tablespoons of oil
½ teaspoon of cumin seeds
1 large onion (finely chopped)

Heat oil in a pan. Add cumin seeds. As soon as they brown, add the onions and fry till nicely browned. Add garlic and all other spices.Stir for a quarter of a minute and mix in the potato pieces.

Cook for about 3 minutes. Add the peppers, mix well, cover and cook on low heat for 8 to 10 minutes (turning them over once or twice). The vegetable should be on the dry side with the oil showing at the top.

Growing up in Mumbai for me was all about having a gang of friends, spending time in each others' homes, gorging on delicious food our mums cooked for the gang (very different from one's own mum of course), chatting for hours, going to the cinema and, later in our teens, sitting in cafes and talking about boys – mostly. My friend Farida had hair so long that she could sit on it. Her mum was also a brilliant cook (I wonder if all women in India are good cooks or I subconsciously chose friends whose mums were great cooks?) and she introduced me to this dish. It was so very delicious with rice. The potato soaked in the aromatic spices and oil, together with the flavoursome peppers, is surely a dish for food aficionados.

Potatoes

Potatoes are a very adaptable entity. You can add them to another vegetable or cook them as a separate dish. Either way they come out tasty. The best potatoes for Indian cooking are of the type that do not disintegrate when cooked. Varieties such as King Edwards, Charlotte, Nicola etc. work well. New potatoes, of course, are always a treat.

PLEASE NOTE:

In Indian cooking, when recipes require boiled potatoes, unless otherwise specified, potatoes are boiled whole in their skin.

PLAIN POTATOES WITH LEMON (Gravy)

Cooking time:
30 minutes

6 medium potatoes (boiled whole in skin)
1 teaspoon of coriander powder
¼ teaspoon of crushed chillies
¼ teaspoon of turmeric powder
¾ teaspoon of salt
3 to 4 tablespoons of lemon juice
3 cups of water
¼ cup of green coriander leaves (chopped)

Baghaar

2 tablespoons of oil
OR 1 tablespoon of ghee or butter
½ teaspoon of cumin seeds
½ teaspoon of asafoetida
2 whole red chillies

Skin the potatoes (if old) and break them roughly into 8 segments each.

Heat the oil / ghee or butter in a pan. Add cumin seeds. When browned, add asafoetida and whole chillis. As soon as they bubble, add the potatoes, other spices and mix gently for 2 to 3 minutes.

Add water and lemon juice. Mix well, cover the pan and let it gently simmer for 10 minutes (there should be enough liquid left to give the vegetable consistency of a thick soup). Garnish with coriander before serving.

This dish can also be prepared by:

1) substituting the lemon juice with 1 large tomato roughly chopped into 8 to 10 pieces.

2) replacing cumin seeds with 1 ½ teaspoons of panch phodani mix

This, in North India, used to be a standard dish at weddings, festivals etc. (and in some parts probably still is, and not replaced by sag paneer, dal makhhani and the likes). It goes well with puris and parathas. In many families, like my great-aunt's, this was the staple evening dish served with other vegetables and parathas - the parathas crispy on the outside and soft as butter inside. I used to love soaking them in the sour, lemony liquid of the potatoes and enjoy every morsel with this mixture of texture and taste.

PLAIN POTATOES (Dry)

Cooking time:
30 minutes

6 medium potatoes (boiled whole in skin)
1½ teaspoons of coriander powder
¼ teaspoon of crushed chillies
¼ teaspoon of turmeric powder
½ teaspoon of salt
½ cup of green coriander leaves (optional)

Baghaar

3 tablespoons of oil
1 teaspoon of cumin seeds
½ teaspoon of asafoetida

Skin the potatoes (if old) and break them roughly into 8 segments each.

Heat oil in a frying pan. Add cumin seeds. When browned, add asafoetida. As soon as it bubbles, add the potatoes and other spices and mix gently and let it sauté for 10 to 12 minutes on a low heat (do not cover the pan). Garnish with coriander before serving.

This dish also can be prepared by:

1) adding 2 tablespoons of lemon juice and a bit extra salt

2) substituting 1 potato with 1 medium tomato roughly chopped into 8 pieces

3) substituting 1 potato with ½ cup of sweet peas.

Train journeys in India (steam engines in my days) were something else! We did quite a few – long ones – as the family was so spread out. Despite the grit and the dirt I used to just love them because life was suspended for a day or two and yet you watched the world go by. As the train progressed on its tracks you got to see the changes in landscape, in people and their clothes but above all in food. Certain places were famous for their specialities such as Lonawala for its Chikki, Muzaffarnagar for Motichoor Laddoos and so on. Don't know how but somehow people knew about these things. For the first night of the journey my mother always packed puris, dry potatoes and pickles. She rarely peeled these potatoes as the vegetable stays better and longer with the skin on. One couldn't ask more of life – eating this simple meal while watching the scenery change every minute. This dish with puris or parathas is perfect for a picnic meal.

POTATOES WITH ONIONS (Dry)

Cooking time:
30 minutes

5 medium potatoes (best with new potatoes)
1½ teaspoons of coriander powder
¼ teaspoon of turmeric powder
¾ teaspoon of salt
1 fresh green chilli (chopped)
½ cup of green coriander leaves (chopped)

Baghaar

6 tablespoons of oil
1 teaspoon of mustard seeds
6 curry leaves
1 large onion (finely chopped)

Boil the potatoes whole in their skins till soft. Skin them (if old) and chop them roughly into small segments.

Heat oil in a frying pan. Add mustard seeds. As soon as they pop, add curry leaves and the onions. Fry till onions are soft and translucent. Add potatoes, green chilli and other spices, mix gently and let it sauté for 10 to 12 minutes on low heat (do not cover the pan). Garnish with coriander before serving.

This dish also can be prepared by:

1) substituting 1 potato with 1 medium tomato roughly chopped into 8 pieces. Mix it in after cooking the potatoes for 8-10 minutes

2) substituting 2 potatoes with 1 medium tomato and ½ cup of peas. Add the peas with the potatoes and mix in the tomato towards the end.

At a bring-a-dish event in London, every last bit of the potato was scraped off the serving dish faster than you could say 'food is served'. Contributed by an Ismaili woman, this was an absolutely delicious dish – mouth wateringly aromatic and with just the right mixture of spices.

POTATOES WITH ONION, TOMATOES AND CASHEW NUTS

Cooking time:
30 minutes

4 medium potatoes (boiled whole in skin)
2 medium tomatoes (finely chopped)
1½ teaspoons of coriander powder
¼ teaspoon of chilli powder
¼ teaspoon of turmeric powder
¾ teaspoon of salt
1 tablespoon of ginger (finely chopped)
1 tablespoon of garlic (finely chopped)
16 cashew nuts
2 cups of water
½ cup of green coriander leaves (chopped)

Baghaar

4 tablespoons of oil
OR 2 tablespoons of ghee or butter
½ teaspoon of cumin seeds
1 large onion (finely chopped)

Skin and chop the potatoes into 4 segments (lengthwise) each.

Heat oil in a pan. Add cumin seeds. As soon as they brown, add the onions and fry till nicely browned. Add ginger, garlic, nuts and all other spices. Stir for a few seconds and add tomatoes.

Simmer for about 5 minutes or till the the liquid has evaporated. Add potatoes and water, mix gently and let it simmer on low heat for approximately 10 minutes.

The dish should have some gravy.

Garnish with coriander before serving.

My sister Bandi is an adventurous cook and often delights the family with her culinary innovation. And like a magpie, I pick what I like from her. This is one of her earlier creations.

POTATOES WITH MIXED NUTS

Cooking time:
30 minutes

20 small potatoes (new)
½ cup of mixed nuts * - (ground rough)
1 teaspoon of coriander powder
½ teaspoon cumin powder
¼ teaspoon of chilli powder
¼ teaspoon of turmeric powder
1 tablespoon of ginger (fine paste)
1 tablespoon of garlic (fine paste)
6 curry leaves
¾ teaspoon of salt
1 cup of milk or water
½ cup green coriander leaves (chopped)

* sesame, peanuts, cashew nuts, coconut
(roughly in same quantity)

Baghaar

2 tablespoons of oil
½ teaspoon of mustard seeds
1 large onion (finely chopped)

Boil potatoes whole in thier skins till soft. Skin them and leave them whole.

Heat oil in a pan. Add mustard seeds. As soon as they pop, add the onions and fry till nicely browned.

Add curry leaves, ginger, garlic, nuts and all other spices. Stir for a quarter of a minute and add milk and potatoes.

Simmer for about 10 minutes on a low heat (the potatoes should be in a thick gravy of nuts, therefore add some liquid - milk or water - if required).

Garnish with coriander before serving.

Credit for this goes to my Gujarati family.

POTATOES WITH TOMATOES (Gravy)

Cooking time:
40 minutes

16 - 20 small potatoes (new)
2 large tomatoes (chopped small)
¼ teaspoon of crushed chillies
1 teaspoon of salt
¼ teaspoon of sugar
1 tablespoon of garlic (paste)
1 cup of water
½ cup of green coriander leaves (chopped)

OIL FOR FRYING

Baghaar

3 tablespoons of ghee/butter
½ teaspoon of cumin seeds
1 large onion (grated)

Skin the potatoes and deep fry them whole in hot oil.

Heat ghee/butter in a pan, add cumin seeds and, when brown, add onions and fry till golden. Stir in all the other spices and garlic.

Add tomatoes, cook till the liquid has evaporated and add potatoes. Stir for a minute or so.

Pour in the water, bring to boil and leave the mixture to simmer for about 10 minutes on low heat (the potatoes should be in a thick gravy of tomatoes; therefore add more water if required).

Mix in the coriander before serving.

This is Manju's recipe. It goes very well with rotis.

POTATOES WITH COCONUT AND PEANUTS (Dry)

Cooking time:
30 minutes

4 medium potatoes (boiled whole in skin)
¼ cup of thin slices of fresh coconut
¼ cup of peanuts (whole)
½ teaspoon of coriander powder
¼ teaspoon of chilli powder
6 curry leaves
¾ teaspoon of salt
½ cup of green coriander leaves (chopped)

Baghaar

4 tablespoons of oil
½ teaspoon of mustard seeds
1 large onion (finely chopped)

Skin potatoes and break them roughly into 6 pieces.

Heat oil in a frying pan. Add mustard seeds. As soon as they pop add the onions and fry till soft and translucent. Add curry leaves, nuts and all other spices. Stir for a few seconds and mix in the potatoes.

Cook for about 10 minutes on a very low heat (without covering). Garnish with fresh coriander before serving.

This dish is often made (but without onions) for one of the many festivals celebrated by the Hindu community. I have added onions for extra flavour.

ALOO DAM

Cooking time:
40 minutes

6 medium potatoes
1 teaspoon of coriander powder
1 teaspoon of garam masala
¼ teaspoon of crushed chillies
¼ teaspoon of turmeric powder
1 tablespoon of garlic (chopped fine)
¾ teaspoon of salt
½ cup of water

Baghaar

8 tablespoons of oil
½ teaspoon of cumin seeds
2 to 3 whole black cardamom
1 small stick cinnamon
2 bay leaves
1 large onion (finely chopped)

Skin and chop the potatoes into 12 pieces each.

Heat oil in a pan. Add cumin seeds. As soon as they brown add bay leaf, cardamom, cinnamon and the onions and fry till nicely browned. Add garlic and all other spices. Stir for a quarter of a minute and mix in the potatoes. Cook for about 3 minutes.

Add water, mix gently and let it simmer on low heat till potatoes are cooked (approximately 10 minutes). The potatoes should be in a thick sauce; therefore add water if required.

The best Aloo Dam I have ever had was sold outside the one and only cinema hall in Baripada. Going to cinema was 'double the pleasure, double the fun' for you not only got to see a movie (sometimes the same one as many as six times if it had a long run – the only cinema hall after all) but also had an array of snacky delights waiting during the interval - peanuts fried in spicy gram flour batter, Chana Chur, boiled peas in hot tamarind sauce and Aloo Dam, all of them sold from a small open stall, and each one so very tempting. But my favourite, above all, remains Aloo Dum, very spicy and hot, each potato piece seeped in a mixture of flavours. This goes well with rice and even better with crunchy puffed rice.

QUICK SERVE POTATOES

Cooking time:
15 minutes

6 medium potatoes
½ teaspoon of coriander powder
¼ teaspoon of crushed chillies
¼ teaspoon of turmeric powder
¾ teaspoon of salt
1 cup of water
2 - 3 tablespoons of lemon juice

Baghaar

2 tablespoons of oil
OR 1 tablespoon of ghee or butter
1 teaspoon of panch phodini
¼ teaspoon of asafoetida

Clean potatoes and chop them, with skins, thin and small (roughly 1cm thick and 3cm long).

Heat oil / ghee or butter in a pan. Add panch phodani, When browned, add asafoetida. As soon as it bubbles, add the potatoes and other spices and mix gently.

Add water and cook till potatoes are tender (about 3 to 4 minutes). Add lemon juice. Mix well and serve.

Some Sundays my naniji used to server this with puris for breakfast

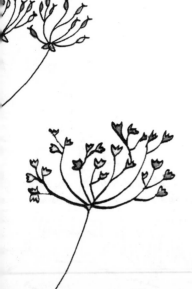

POTATOES WITH BLACK PEPPER (Dry)

Cooking time:
30 minutes

6 medium potatoes (boiled in skin)
¾ teaspoon of crushed black pepper
¾ teaspoon of salt

Baghaar

6 tablespoons of oil
½ teaspoon of cumin seeds
¼ teaspoon of asafoetida

Skin potatoes and chop them into 4 pieces each (lengthwise).

Heat oil in a frying pan. Add cumin seeds. When browned, add asafoetida. As soon as it bubbles, add the potatoes and mix gently. Cook on low heat till potatoes are brown (approx. 10 minutes). Add salt and pepper.

Mix well, cook for another 2 to 3 minutes and serve.

Our Sindhi friends used to serve this as a snack with drinks.

POTATOES WITH GARLIC AND PAPRIKA (Dry)

Cooking time:
15 - 20 minutes

6 medium potatoes
1 teaspoon of coriander powder
¼ teaspoon of chilli powder
1½ teaspoons of paprika
2 tablespoons of garlic (paste)
¾ teaspoon of salt
¼ cup of water
½ cup green coriander leaves (chopped)

Baghaar

6 tablespoons of oil
½ teaspoon of cumin seeds

Skin potatoes and cut them into 4 segments (lengthwise).

Heat oil in a frying pan. Add cumin seeds. When browned, add garlic and all other spices. Stir for a few seconds and add the potatoes. Mix and stir for a minute.

Add water. Mix well, cover the pan and let it gently simmer for 5 to 7 minutes (or till the potatoes are cooked and all water has evaporated). Garnish with coriander before serving.

One of my creations.

SOUTH INDIAN STYLE POTATOES

Cooking time:
15 - 20 minutes

4 medium potatoes (boiled in skin)
1 large onion (sliced rough in medium size pieces)
1 medium tomato (chopped small)
1 teaspoon of coriander powder
¼ teaspoon of chilli powder
¼ teaspoon of tumeric powder
1 small green chilli (chopped fine)
¾ teaspoon of salt
¼ cup of water
½ cup green coriander leaves (chopped)

Baghaar

4 tablespoons of oil
1 teaspoon of mustard seeds
1 tablespoon urad dal
6 - 8 curry leaves

Skin the potatoes (if old) and break them roughly into 6 to 8 segments each.

Heat oil in a frying pan. Add mustard seeds and urad dal. As soon as they pop add curry leaves, onions and all other spices including the green chilli. Toss for a few seconds and the add potatoes, mix gently, cover and let it cook for 8 to 10 minutes on low heat.

Add tomatoes and water, mix and cook for a further 2 or 3 minutes. Garnish with coriander before serving.

These potatoes are simply perfect with dosas or with sambhar and rice.

PUMPKIN SWEET AND SOUR

Cooking time:
15 - 20 minutes

½ kg of pumpkin
(if hard skin, peeled, and chopped into small pieces)
½ teaspoon of coriander powder
¼ teaspoon of crushed chillies
¼ teaspoon of turmeric
¾ teaspoon of salt
2 to 3 teaspoons of sugar
3 to 4 tablespoons of lemon juice

Baghaar

1 tablespoon of oil
½ teaspoon of fenugreek seeds
½ teaspoon of cumin seeds
½ teaspoon of asafoetida

Heat oil in a pan. Add fenugreek seeds and, when they pop, add cumin seeds and asafoetida. When browned, add pumpkin and all other ingredients (except sugar and lemon juice).

Stir well, cover and cook on low heat for 5 to 7 minutes. Add sugar and lemon juice, and cook for another 2 to 3 minutes.

The vegetable should not be too dry, therefore; add a few spoons of water if necessary.

To this day, after all her travels, this vegetable remains much loved by my mother . She always serves this with Punjabi kaddhi – another of her favourite dishes. She cooked up these two dishes more often than the family could humanly appreciate. It's only after moving to the UK did I learn to savour the subtle sweet taste combined with slight tanginess from the lemon and a hint of bitter aroma from fenugreek. I usually serve this with lemony potatoes, other vegetables, kachoris and puris for the festival of Diwali.

PUMPKIN WITH ONIONS

Cooking time:
15 - 20 minutes

½ kg of pumpkin
(if hard skin, peeled, and chopped into 5 to 6 cm pieces)
1 teaspoon of coriander powder
¼ teaspoon of crushed chillies
¼ teaspoon of turmeric
¾ teaspoon of salt
1 bunch of fresh dill or ½ cup of dry dill
(soaked in water)

Baghaar

4 tablespoons of oil
½ teaspoon of fenugreek seeds
1 medium onion (chopped into chunky pieces)

Heat oil in a frying pan. Add fenugreek seeds. As soon as they brown, add the onions and fry till nicely browned. Add all the other spices and pumpkin.

Mix well, and cook (without cover) on medium heat for 4 to 5 minutes. Add dill and cook for another 2 to 3 minutes. (Turn vegetables over once or twice but ensure that the pumpkin does not overcook and go mushy).

The vegetable should be dry, the pumpkin brown and crispy.

In Mumbai I had the opportunity to meet people from all over India (and a few from Europe), and enjoy their food. London offered me the chance to meet people from all over the world, make friends with them and relish their food. In this international community of friends, there were people of Indian ancestry who were born and brought up in different corners of the world such as Trinidad, Kenya and South Africa. Their cuisine, while keeping to the region of India their forebears came from, is heavily influenced by the place they grew up in. This is such a bonus as it further adds to the variety and tastes. This recipe is from one such friend, Bibi, from Guyana. We lived next door to each other and regularly passed our speciality food over the fence. (Incidentally we did this with our children too. Her son and my daughter were born just a few months apart. As babies they also got passed over the fence when Bibi or I needed a little break). With this pumpkin dish Bibi also supplied dal-rotis, which needless to say are a perfect companion to it. To this day my children cannot eat one without the other. However, it is very flavoursome and goes very well with rice and dal too.

PUMPKIN WITH YOGHURT

Cooking time:
15 - 20 minutes

½ kg of pumpkin
(peeled, and chopped into 5 to 6cm pieces)
¼ cup of water
500g of thick yoghurt (preferably Greek style)
½ teaspoon of salt
6 whole cloves
1 medium clove of garlic (finely chopped)

Baghaar

8 tablespoons of oil
¼ teaspoon of chilli powder
½ teaspoon of paprika

Place the pumpkin in a shallow pan, big enough so that most of the pieces fit in at the bottom of the pan. Sprinkle the cloves and garlic over the pumpkin. Mix the salt in the water and pour this over as well.

Put the pot on high heat and bring the mixture to boil. Lower the heat and cook for 2 to 3 minutes (pumpkin should be tender but not too soft).

Transfer the pumpkin onto a serving dish. Heat the oil in a pan, turn the heat off and mix in the chilli and paprika. Pour this over the pumpkin (all this can be done in advance and the pumpkin warmed again just before layering the yoghurt). Smooth the yoghurt, pour it evenly over the pumpkin and serve.

Recently, after wandering around a trendy area of London with my sakhis, we came across an Afghani café and decided to have lunch. While all the food we decided to try was nice, this dish was heavenly. I have cooked this often for family and friends and to date all have loved it. I think it is the subtle aroma of garlic and cloves combined with the sweetness of pumpkin and the creamy tartness of yoghurt that works like magic.

SPINACH WITH POTATOES

Cooking time:
15 - 20 minutes

½ kg spinach (if fresh, chopped small and simmered down)*
1 medium potato (peeled and chopped into 8 pieces)
¾ teaspoon of coriander powder
¼ teaspoon of crushed chillies
¼ teaspoon of turmeric
½ teaspoon of salt

Baghaar

2 tablespoons of oil
½ teaspoon of cumin seeds
½ teaspoon of asafoetida

* If using other than fresh spinach, the frozen-leafy kind is the best.

Heat oil in a wok. Add cumin seeds and asafoetida. When browned add potatoes, spinach and all other ingredients.

Stir well, cover and cook on low heat for 5 to 7 minutes. Toss the vegetables on a high heat for a minute or two or till all water has evaporated.

This dish can be cooked with garlic:
Add one teaspoon of chopped garlic instead of asafoetida

One can also replace potatoes with chunky pieces of tomatoes – added towards the end of the cooking process.

Spinach is a very flavoursome vegetable. A number of my European friends said that they had always hated spinach till they tasted it cooked Indian style. Spinach with potatoes is another simple, healthy recipe from my naniji's kitchen.

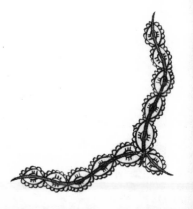

SPINACH WITH GARLIC

Cooking time:
15 - 20 minutes

½ kg of spinach
(blended to a paste - if fresh, simmered down first)
1 teaspoon of coriander powder
¼ teaspoon of chilli powder
½ teaspoon of salt

Baghaar

4 tablespoons of butter / ghee
½ teaspoon of cumin seeds
2 teaspoons of garlic (paste)
1 teaspoon of paprika powder

Heat a quarter of the butter/ghee in a pan. Add cumin seeds. As soon they brown, stir in 1 teaspoon of garlic. Cook till brown.

Add spinach and all the other spices (except paprika). Mix well and cover the pan. Cook on gentle heat for 5 minutes and then on high till all water has evaporated.

Before serving, heat the rest of the butter/ghee, stir in remaining garlic and brown it. Turn the heat off, mix in the paprika and pour the mixture on top of the spinach.

In my school, the gang I hung around with used to share the food we brought in for lunch. A Sindhi friend used to occasionally bring spinach cooked this way, and we ate it with paper thin rotis. All I can say about the taste is wow! The important thing is the butter/ghee on top of the vegetable – it gives the spinach an exceptional taste and flavour.

SPINACH WITH CREAM

Cooking time:
15 - 20 minutes

½ kg of spinach
(if fresh, chopped small & simmered down)
1 teaspoon of coriander powder
½ teaspoon of garam masala
¼ teaspoon of crushed chillies
1 tablespoon of garlic (finely chopped)
½ teaspoon of salt
½ cup of thick cream

Baghaar

1 tablespoon of butter or ghee
½ teaspoon of cumin seeds
1 large onion (finely chopped)

Heat butter/ghee in a good size pan. Add cumin seeds and, when browned, mix in the onions. Fry gently till translucent.

Add coriander, garam masala and crushed chillies. Simmer for few seconds and add spinach, garlic and salt. Mix well and cover the pan.

Leave to cook till most of the water from the spinach has evaporated. Add the cream and simmer for 1 to 2 minutes.

This dish can be made with paneer:
Add ½ cup of fried paneer cubes together with spinach

This dish can also be made without cream:
Add ¾ cup of fried paneer cubes together with spinach and leave the cream out altogether.

I was surprised to find that in Britain a lot of people hate spinach. I once cooked this for a dinner party in London. One of my friends could not have enough of it and later said that she intensely dislikes spinach but did not realize that that's what she was eating till towards the end of the meal. This is a very rich dish but, like all things that are not so good for us, is delicious. However, rich food is not something any of us cook on a daily basis – such indulgences are for the weekend or parties.

SWEET CORN WITH COURGETTE AND NUTS

Cooking time:
15 - 20 minutes

¼ kg of corn (frozen variety is better than tin)
1 medium courgette (chopped into very small pieces)
¼ cup of cashew nuts (broken into half)
¼ teaspoon of crushed chillies
½ teaspoon of salt
½ cup of green coriander leaves (chopped)
OR any other herb

Baghaar

3 tablespoons of oil
1 medium onion (finely chopped)

Heat the oil in a pan, add the onions and fry till translucent. Add the nuts and brown them. Mix in the courgette and all other spices. Stir for a minute or two.

Add the corn, mix well, cover and cook on low heat for 5 to 7 minutes, turning them over once or twice.

The vegetable should be dry. Before serving, sprinkle with coriander.

This dish can be cooked with any vegetable, including potatoes.

This dish can be cooked with ½ cup of sauted paneer instead of courgette.

They say that necessity is the mother of invention – so true. This was another of my brain waves when trying to feed a family on the limited number of vegetables around and, more importantly, with limited finances. This goes very well with pitta bread and crunchy salad.

CORN ON COB WITH NUTS

Cooking time:
15 - 20 minutes

4 - 6 pieces (6 to 8 cm long) corn on cob
(if fresh cobs boil them first)
1 cup of mixed nuts* (ground smooth)
1 teaspoon of coriander powder
¼ teaspoon of cumin powder
¼ teaspoon of chilli powder
1 tablespoon of garlic (paste)
¾ teaspoon of salt
1 cup of water
½ cup of green coriander leaves (chopped)

Baghaar

3 tablespoons of oil
½ teaspoon of mustard seeds
1 large onion (finely chopped)
6-8 curry leaves

* mainly peanuts, coconut, sesame seeds and any other
nuts on hand.

Heat oil in a pan. Add cumin seeds. As soon as they brown, add
the onions and fry till nicely browned. Add garlic, curry leaves
and all other spices. Stir for a few seconds. Add water and cook for
about 3 minutes.

Add the corn, mix well, cover and cook on low heat for 8 - 10
minutes, turning them over once or twice. The vegetable should
have a nice thick sauce (add extra water if necessary).

Before serving sprinkle with coriander.

*As you can imagine, this is a bit messy to eat but truly worth the mess. The
cobs soak in all the spice and nut flavours and in every bite you get that
aromatic sensation, together with that unique taste of corn drenched in the
nutty sauce. Great on its own or with rice.*

TOMATOES IN COCONUT (Kerala)

Cooking time:
15 - 20 minutes

6 medium tomatoes
1 cup of coconut milk
OR 4 tablespoons of coconut cream with ½ cup of water
¾ teaspoon of coriander powder
¼ teaspoon of chilli powder
½ teaspoon of salt
¼ cup of green coriander leaves (chopped)

Baghaar

1 tablespoon of oil
1 tablespoon of mustard seeds
1 tablespoon of garlic (chopped fine)
4 - 6 curry leaves

Like potatoes, tomatoes are excellent on their own but are used mainly for enhancing other vegetables. Here are some of my favourite recipes

Pour the boiling water on the tomatoes and leave for 10 minutes. Skin the tomatoes and leave them whole.

Heat the oil in a pan and add mustard seeds. As soon as they pop, add garlic, curry leaves, and all the other spices. Stir for a quarter of a minute, add coconut milk (or coconut cream with water), bring to boil and mix in the tomatoes.

Cook for about 3 to 4 minutes on low heat (the tomatoes should remain firm). Sprinkle with coriander and serve.

While gliding over the tranquil back waters, in Kerala in a rice-boat (converted into a total comfort zone for two), and eating almost non-stop delights the cook conjured up, I am surprised I had the presence of mind to ask him for the recipe for this dish. You have to try this to understand why I must have come out of the scenery and food induced stupor to somehow write the recipe down .

TOMATOES WITH DESICCATED COCONUT (Maharashtran)

Cooking time:
30 minutes

8 small tomatoes (or 400g tinned)
½ cup of desiccated coconut
OR 4 tablespoons of coconut cream
½ teaspoon of garam masala
¼ teaspoon of turmeric powder
1 teaspoon of garlic (paste)
1 cup of water
½ teaspoon of sugar
1 teaspoon of coriander powder
¼ teaspoon of chilli powder
1 teaspoon of ginger (paste)
6 curry leaves
¾ teaspoon of salt
½ cup of green coriander leaves (chopped)

Baghaar

2 tablespoons of oil
½ teaspoon of mustard seeds
1 large onion (finely chopped)

Pour boiling water on the tomatoes and leave for 10 minutes. Skin them and leave them whole. With tinned tomatoes, use straight from the tin.

Heat the oil in a pan and add mustard seeds. As soon as they pop, add the onions and fry till nicely browned. Add curry leaves, ginger, garlic, coconut and all other spices. Stir for a quarter of a minute. Add one cup of water and cook for 5 minutes on low heat.

Add tomatoes and simmer for about 5 to 7 minutes on a low heat (the tomatoes should remain firm and be in a thick gravy, therefore add some water if required). Garnish with coriander before serving.

It's very difficult to find regional vegetarian food in Goa. Last year, we did a family holiday, with my brother from New Zealand, my sister from London, our partners and children. All of us are committed vegetarians. So we searched high and low for some Goanese/ Maharashtran vegetarian food and came across this cafe run by a woman who cooks only on order. One has to ring her in advance and book. She then tells you what options are possible from the menu and takes about three-quarters of an hour to get it all ready for you. You have to believe me when I say – it is definitely worth the rigmarole. The food was fresh, the vegetables seasonal, and every dish totally satisfying. But the tomato dish was my favourite. This wonderful chef served it with very thick dal, other vegetables and rice. It also goes together well with sprouted mung.

TOMATOES STUFFED WITH PANEER

Cooking time:
40 minutes

4 large tomatoes
1 cup of paneer (grated or crumbled)
1 teaspoon of coriander powder
½ teaspoon of garam masala
¼ teaspoon of chilli powder
¼ teaspoon of turmeric powder
¾ teaspoon of salt
½ cup of green coriander leaves (chopped)

Baghaar

4 tablespoons of oil
½ teaspoon of cumin seeds
1 teaspoon of garlic (finely chopped)
1 medium onion (finely chopped)

Thinly slice the tops of the tomatoes, scoop out the inside and rub the outside with oil (The scooped out tomatoes can be used for another dish).

Heat 3 tablespoons of oil in a frying pan. Add cumin seeds. As soon as they brown add the onions and fry till nicely browned. Add garlic, all the other spices and half of the green coriander. Stir for a few seconds and add paneer. Cook for 5 minutes on low heat and leave it to cool.

Divide the paneer mix into 4 portions and stuff the tomatoes with it. Close the tomatoes with sliced tops. Pour the remaining oil into the pan and heat it gently. Place the tomatoes in the hot oil, cover the pan and cook for 5 minutes OR grease an oven dish with the remaining oil, place the tomatoes in it and cook them in a hot oven for 10 to 15 minutes. Sprinkle with fresh coriander and serve.

Years ago when I was in the hospital, having had my second child and completely fed up with the bland food provided in the maternity ward, my sister, Bandi, turned into a food angel and saved me from the misery. Aware of my partiality to dairy products, she rustled up different paneer dishes every day - paneer paratha, paneer stuffed tomatoes. Try it with pulao rice. It is just scrumptious.

Rice

Rice comes in many varieties. The taste, flavour, texture, size and cooking time all vary depending on the type and quality of the rice. For the sake of keeping it simple, and because it is really easy to cook, I have used basmati rice for all the recipes.

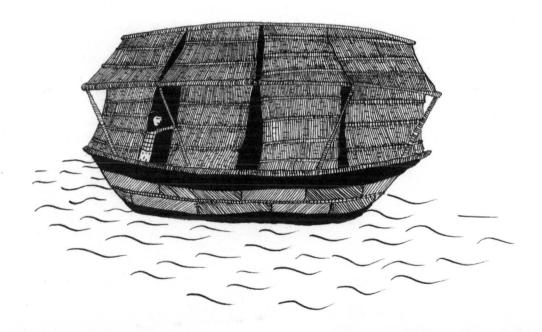

Measurements:

All recipes are for 4 people. If you are serving a combination of rice and some kind of bread you will need to use less rice than specified. Adjust the measurement of water accordingly.

For Best Results:

For rice to have a finish where the grains separate nicely and do not turn mushy, it is best to:

- Wash the rice till the water runs clear.

- Soak it for 10 to 15 minutes in the required amount of water.

- Cook the rice in the soaked water to keep all the nutrients in.

Also:

- It is best not to boil rice in extra water. When the rice is cooked thus and the excess water is drained, it leaves the rice with a very bland taste. Also, most of the nutrients are lost in the process.

- A sign that the rice is ready, is when holes appear at the top of the cooking rice and the sides look dry. This generally takes 10 to 12 minutes on a low heat, after the rice has come to boil.

PLAIN RICE

Cooking time:
15 - 20 minutes

**1½ cups of rice
3 cups of water**

Wash the rice till the water runs clear. Soak it in 3 cups of water for 10 to 15 minutes. Place it on a high heat till it comes to the boil. Lower the heat to minimum and cook for 10 to 12 minutes or till all water is dried out. If the rice feels raw, sprinkle 1 or 2 spoons of hot water and leave on heat for few more minutes.

This rice works with almost any dal, beans and / or vegetables .

You can add a pinch of turmeric and, if preferred, salt.

For extra flavour - add ½ tablespoon of ghee or butter at the boiling stage.

For extra, extra flavour - add a few pods of either cardamom or cloves or a small piece of cinnamon or 1 bay leaf; or all; or any combination of these!

My family is originally from North India where rice is eaten occasionally. It is a wheat growing region so the staple is flat bread in a variety of forms. However, to my father's consternation, rather than bread I actually favour rice. He always used to lament "what kind of Punjabi are you?" Perhaps this partiality for rice is due to being born and spending much time in Baripada where rice is eaten for breakfast, lunch and dinner in some form or other. Even now, after living for forty years in Britain, when I am tired and very hungry, the only thing that really satisfies my hunger is rice with plain dal and pickle – no trimmings whatsoever are required.

FRIED RICE

Cooking time:
15 - 20 minutes

1½ cups of rice
½ teaspoon of salt
2½ cups of water

Baghaar

1 tablespoon of ghee or butter
1 teaspoon of cumin seeds

Wash the rice till the water runs clear. Soak it for 10 to 15 minutes. Put the rice in a sieve and drain the water out completely.

Heat the ghee in a good size pan, add cumin, and, when it pops, put the rice in. Stir gently (on medium heat) till the rice turns slightly pink.

Mix in 2½ cups of boiling water and salt. Lower the heat to the minimum and cook for 10 to 12 minutes till all the water is dried out. In case the rice feels raw, sprinkle one or 2 tablespoons of hot water and leave on the heat for few more minutes.

Fried rice can be made with:

onions – fry 1 finely diced onion with cumin (before adding rice)

whole spices such as cardamom etc. can be added together with cumin

dried onion flakes can be browned in a small amount of ghee/butter and spread on top of cooked rice.

VEGETABLE PULAO

Cooking time:
15 - 20 minutes

1½ cups of rice
½ cup of vegetable/s diced small *
¾ teaspoon of salt
2 cups of water

Baghaar

1½ tablespoons of ghee or butter
1 small onion diced small
whole spices of choice

Wash the rice till the water runs clear. Soak it for 10 to 15 minutes. Put it in a sieve and drain the water out completely.

Heat the ghee in a good size pan, add the onions and, when brown, mix in the whole spices and rice. Stir gently (on a medium heat) till the rice turns pink.

Add the vegetable/s. Stir for a minute and mix in 2 cups of boiling water and lower the heat to the minimum. Cook for 10 to 12 minutes till all the water is dried out. In case the rice feels raw, sprinkle 1 or 2 tablespoons of hot water and leave on the heat for a few more minutes.

The vegetable/s can be substituted with:

¼ cup of lentil (chana, moong, or toor) soaked in hot water for ½ hour.

½ cup of paneer chopped into very small pieces - when the onions have browned - sauté the paneer for a few minutes before adding the rice.

½ cup of whole or split almonds or cashew nuts - add these with onions and brown them together.

* One or more seasonal vegetables - cauliflower, beans, peppers, peas. But peas, carrots and corn together make a wonderful colour combination with the white of the rice.

KHICHRI

Cooking time:
15 - 20 minutes

1 cup of rice
¼ plain moong dal or moong dal with skin
(split whole moong)
½ teaspoon of tumeric
½ teaspoon of salt
4 cups of water

Wash the rice and dal till the water runs clear. Soak it in 4 cups of water for 10 to 15 minutes. Cook on a high heat till it comes to the boil. Add the salt and turmeric, lower the heat to the minimum and cook for 10 to 15 minutes till all the water is dried out. The rice should feel soft, and the texture should be moist.

Khichri is extremely nutritive and easy to digest thus, together with boiled vegetables, it makes a healthy meal for an ill or convalescing person. To make a real meal of it, the saying goes, Khichri needs 4 friends – yoghurt, papad, ghee and pickle. Tomato chutney also is a good accompaniment.

Breads

I have yet to see anyone not like freshly made Indian breads. Children especialy love rotis and puris and are liable to eat them as snacks. Rotis or parathas fresh off the tawa and puris puffed up into a hot ball go like 'hot cakes' so if you are providing them fresh then be prepared for people to polish off more than you would expect.

In general, the flour used for making Indian bread, in effect is whole meal wheat flour milled to a specific consistency. Unless otherwise specified use medium or fine chapatti flour for rotis, puris and parathas. If chapatti flour is not available a ½ and ½ mix of good quality whole meal flour and plain flour should do the trick.

Dough ought to be kneaded well by folding it over and over inwards. The amount of water required may vary according to the properties of the flour.

When making the bread, if for some reason, the dough is too soft to manage, just knead in sufficient dry flour to give it the desired consistency to roll.

All these breads are best served fresh but they can be prepared in advance (especially for a party) and warmed before serving The amount of flour specified for the recipes here will be sufficient for 4 people, ONLY if accompanied with rice. If only serving bread increase the amount of flour to 1½ cup and increase all other ingredients accordingly.

My family and friends - and me - tend to somewhat overeat when fresh rotis, parathas etc. are served, so I always make extra rather than the exact amount. Of course the leftovers are a real treat too – I love a breakfast of the previous night's rotis/parathas and vegetables. They can also be frozen for a later date.

Roti

Roti is the simplest basic Indian bread that can be eaten for breakfast, lunch and dinner. To get best results:

- Use a heavy iron tawa (griddle pan) or heavy-duty frying pan.

- Sit the dough for half an hour at least.

- Make sure the tawa/pan is really hot before starting the roti

PLAIN ROTI

Cooking time:
15 - 20 minutes

1 cup flour
½ cup water
¼ cup flour (for coating the dough balls)
2 teaspoons ghee or butter

Mix 1 cup flour with small amounts of water at a time and knead dough which is springy.

Leave the dough covered with a damp cloth for at least ½ hour (dough can be made well in advance). Divide it into 8 balls.

Place tawa on heat (above medium). Coat the ball of dough with dry flour and roll into a round shape (approximately 1mm thick).

Put the roti on the hot tawa, (while waiting for it to cook start rolling the next one). Give it 20 sec. or so and flip the roti on tawa to other side. Again give it 20 seconds and flip back.

With a napkin or rolled up tissue gently press the roti from the centre to the edge. Flip to the other side (the top side – with thinner layer - should be well browned).

Roast the bottom for 30 seconds and take it off the tawa. Spread ¼ tea spoon of butter or ghee on the top side.

SINDHI CHAPATTI

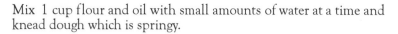

Cooking time:
15 - 20 minutes

1 cup flour
½ cup water
1 ½ table spoon oil
¼ cup flour (for coating the dough balls)
3 teaspoons ghee or butter

Mix 1 cup flour and oil with small amounts of water at a time and knead dough which is springy.

Leave the dough covered for at least ½ hour (dough can be made well in advance). Divide it into 8 balls.

Place tawa on heat (above medium). Coat the ball of dough with dry flour and roll into small oval shape. Pinch in the middle (making 2 round shapes) and dab a bit of ghee on one side and press the other on top (giving it a flat round shape).

Roll out into a round shape (approximately 1mm thick). Put the roti on the hot tawa (while waiting for it to cook start rolling the next one). Give it 20 seconds or so and flip the roti on tawa to other side. Again give it 20 seconds and flip back.

With a napkin or rolled up tissue gently press the roti from the centre to the edges. Flip to the other side.

Roast the bottom for 30 seconds and take it off the tawa. Spread ¼ tea spoon of butter or ghee on the top side.

GUJARATI ROTALI

Cooking time:
15 - 20 minutes

1 cup flour
½ cup water
2 tablespoon oil
¼ cup flour (for coating the dough balls)
3 teaspoons ghee or butter

Mix 1 cup flour with oil and with small amounts of water at a time knead dough which is springy.

Leave the dough covered for at least ½ hour (dough can be made well in advance). Divide it into 10 balls.

Place tawa on heat (above medium). Coat the ball of dough with dry flour and roll into paper thin round shape (approximately ½ mm thick).

Put the roti on the hot tawa (while waiting for it to cook start rolling the next one). Give it 20 sec or so and flip the roti on to other side. Again give it 20 seconds and flip back.

With a napkin or rolled up tissue gently press the roti from the centre to the edge. Flip to the other side (the top side – with thinner layer - should be well browned).

Roast the bottom for 30 seconds and take it off the tawa. Spread ¼ tea spoon of butter or ghee on the top side.

PURANPURI (Gujarati/Maharashtran)

Cooking time:
40 minutes

1 cup flour
2 table spoons oil
½ cup water
¼ cup flour (for coating the dough balls)
8 teaspoons ghee or butter

Filling

½ cup toor
OR chana dal
(soaked for at least 1 hour)
¾ cup sugar
crushed seeds of 4 cardamom (optional)

Filling: Boil the dal in ½ cup of water until it is a soft mush. Mix in the sugar and cardamom and continue cooking it till the mixture turns to dry paste. When cold divide into 8 balls.

Knead the flour with oil and water into a springy dough and divide it into 8 balls.

Place tawa on heat (just above medium). Coat the ball of dough with dry flour and roll into small round shape.

Place the filling in the centre and bring the edges together and squeeze at the top. Coat this with dry flour and gently roll out into a round shape (approximately 1mm thick).

Put the roti on the hot tawa (while waiting for it to cook start rolling the next one). Give the roti on tawa 20 sec. or so and using a spatula flip to other side. Again give it 20 seconds and flip back.

With a napkin or rolled up tissue gently press the roti on the edges. Flip to the other side (the top side – with thinner layer - should be well browned).

Roast the bottom for 30 seconds and take it off the tawa. Spread 1 tea spoon of ghee/butter on the top side.

The Gujaratis generally make this roti with toor dal and the Maharashtrans with chana. Both serve it with main meal, however, I prefer it for afters.

MISSI ROTI

Cooking time:
15 - 20 minutes

½ cup flour
½ cup gram flour
½ cup water
1 tablespoon oil
½ teaspoon salt
1 green chilli (finely chopped)
OR ½ tea spoon rough ground black pepper
¼ cup flour (for coating the dough balls)
2 tea spoons ghee or butter

Follow the plain roti method.

Missi roti can also be made with finely chopped onions. Add 1 small finely chopped onion when making the dough and use less water.

This roti is really nice for breakfast with chai.

DAL ROTI

Cooking time:
40 minutes

½ cup whole moong (soaked for at least 2 hours)
½ cup flour
1 tablespoon oil
½ teaspoon salt
¼ cup flour (for coating the dough balls)
4 teaspoons ghee or butter

Boil moong in 1 cup of water and mush it into a soft dry paste. When cold, mix all ingredients and knead dough which is springy. Divide it into 8 balls.

Place tawa on heat (just above medium). Coat the ball of dough with dry flour and gently roll out into round shape (approximately 1 mm thick).

Put the roti on the hot tawa (while waiting for it to cook start rolling the next one). Give it 20 sec. or so and flip to other side. Again give it 20 seconds and flip back.

With a napkin or rolled up tissue gently press the roti from the centre to the edge. Flip to the other side (The top side – with thinner layer - should be well browned).

Roast the bottom for 30 seconds and take it off the tawa. Spread ½ tea spoon of ghee on the top side.

Paste of ginger, garlic and chilli can also added to the dough.

This roti goes well with any vegetable. Full of nutrition, it can also be used as a snack. This is also a clever way of using up leftover dal.

Paratha

Paratha is a shallow fried bread and can be mutli-layered or stuffed. The layered ones can be a traditional triangle shape or a square or even round.

PARATHA (PLAIN)

Cooking time:
30 minutes

1 cup flour
½ cup water
1 tablespoon oil
¼ cup flour (for coating the dough balls)
10 teaspoons ghee or butter
(for shallow frying)

Mix 1 cup flour with oil and small amounts of water at a time and knead dough which is springy. Leave the dough covered for at least ½ hour (dough can be made well in advance). Divide it in 8 balls.

Melt ghee/butter in a small bowl. Place tawa on heat (just above medium). Coat the ball of dough with dry flour and roll into very thin round shape. Dip a spoon in melted ghee and thinly apply on rolled out dough. Fold in half. Apply ghee again and fold into a triangle.

Coat this with dry flour and gently roll out into triangular shape (approximately 1mm thick). Put the paratha on the hot tawa, (while waiting for it to cook start rolling the next one). Give it 20 sec. or so and flip to other side.

Coat it liberally with ghee. Again give it 20 seconds and flip back and coat the other side with ghee. With a spoon gently press the paratha on the edges. Flip to the other side.

Both sides should be well browned so the outside is crispy while the inner layers are soft.

For square shaped parathas: coat the ball of dough with dry flour and roll into very thin round shape. Thinly apply ghee and fold in half. Apply ghee again and fold into a strip. Apply ghee one more time and overlap the end bits of the strip so as to form a square and then roll this out into a paratha.

For round shaped parathas: coat the ball of dough with dry flour and roll into very thin round shape. Thinly apply ghee and roll it up into a scroll. Apply ghee to the side and fold into a round spiral and then roll this out into a paratha.

AJWAIN PARATHA

Cooking time:
30 minutes

1 cup flour
½ cup water

2 tablespoons oil
½ teaspoon salt
½ teaspoon of ajwain or oregano
¼ cup flour (for coating the dough balls)
10 tea spoons ghee or butter
(for shallow frying)

For cooking follow the plain paratha method.

PARATHA (Stuffed)

Cooking time:
45 minutes

1 cup flour
½ cup water
1 tablespoon oil
½ teaspoon salt
¼ cup flour (for coating the dough balls)
8 tea spoons ghee or butter
(for shallow frying)

Filling

2 large potatoes
(boiled whole in skin then skinned and mashed)
1 green chilli (finely chopped)
OR ½ tea spoon rough ground black pepper
½ cup green coriander leaves (finely chopped)
½ teaspoon salt

The best aloo paratha I have ever enjoyed was in a
dhabba (roadside eatery) between Brindaban and Delhi.
The guy cooked the top layer beatifully crisp with the
soft mushy filling, fragrant with butter and chilli.

Mix flour with oil, salt and small amounts of water at a time and knead dough which is springy. Leave the dough covered for at least ½ hour (dough can be made well in advance). Divide it in 10 balls.

Mix all the filling ingredients well together and divide into 10 equal portions. Place tawa on heat (just above medium). Coat the ball of dough with dry flour and roll into small round shape. Place the filling in the centre and bring the edges together and squeeze at the top.

Coat this with dry flour and gently roll out into round shape (approximately 1mm thick). Put the paratha on the hot tawa, (while waiting for it to cook start rolling the next one) Give it 20 sec. or so and flip to other side. Coat it liberally with ghee. Again give it 20 seconds and flip back and coat the other side with ghee.

With a spoon gently press the paratha on the edges. Flip to the other side. Both sides should be well browned.

The above can be made with other fillings such as cauliflower, paneer or dal.

Cauliflower Filling: in oil fry 1 medium finely chopped onion then add 1 small finely chopped cauliflower. Mix in 1 table spoon of ginger paste and salt. Cook till cauliflower is mushy and dry. When cold mix in green chilli and fresh coriander.

Paneer Filling: replace potatoes with 2 cups of crumbled (if home made) or grated (if ready made) paneer (paneer can be also prepared like the cauliflower filling).

Dal Filling: ½ cup chana dal (soaked for at least 1 hour). Boil the dal in ½ cup of water. Mush it and cook until it turns into a soft dry dough. As in potato paratha, add all other ingredients (this can be also made as a roti).

ONION PARATHA / THEPLA

Cooking time:
30 minutes

1 cup flour
¼ cup water
2 tablespoons oil
½ teaspoon salt
1 medium onion – finely chopped
1 green chilli finely chopped
OR ½ teaspoon rough ground black pepper
½ cup green coriander leaves (finely chopped)
¼ cup flour (for coating the dough balls)
4 teaspoons ghee
OR butter
OR oil for shallow frying

Mix flour, 2 spoons of oil, salt, onion and chilli then with small amounts of water knead dough which is springy. Divide it into 8 balls.

Place tawa on heat (just above medium). Coat the ball of dough with dry flour and gently roll out into round shape (approximately 1mm thick). Prick it in 5 to 6 places with a knife point.

Put the paratha on the hot tawa (while waiting for it to cook start rolling the next one). Give it 20 sec. or so and flip to other side. Coat it liberally with ghee/oil. Again give it 20 seconds and flip back and coat the other side with ghee/oil. With a spoon gently press the paratha on the edges. Flip to the other side. Both sides should be well browned.

In the above onion can be substituted with:

1 cup of grated white radish (muli): when using muli you will not need water to make the dough as muli has natural water.

With green fenugreek (metthi) leaves: Onion can also be substituted with 2 cups of green fenugreek leaves – pluck the leaves from stalk, wash and chop fine.

This makes a good tea time snack for children. Once we had our German friends visiting us in London. I prepared a picnic lunch consisting of a variety of theplas, raita, chutneys etc. Sitting in Hyde Park with this aromatic spread was great fun. Our friends found this so much better than sandwiches.

SWEET PARATHA

Cooking time:
30 minutes

1 cup flour
½ cup water
2 tablespoons oil
8 tablespoons sugar
8 teaspoons ghee/ butter
(for shallow frying)

Mix 1 cup flour with oil and small amounts of water at a time and knead dough which is springy. Leave the dough covered for at least ½ hour (dough can be made well in advance). Divide it in 8 balls.

Place tawa on heat (just above medium). Coat the ball of dough with dry flour and roll into very thin round shape. Thinly apply ghee, sprinkle ½ table spoon of sugar and fold into half. Apply ghee again, sprinkle another ½ spoon of sugar and fold into a triangle.

Coat this with dry flour and gently roll out into triangular shape (approximately 1mm thick). Put the paratha on the hot tawa (while waiting for it to cook start rolling the next one). Give it 20 sec. or so and flip to other side. Coat it liberally with ghee. Again give it 20 seconds and flip back and coat the other side with ghee. With a spoon gently press the paratha on the edges. Flip to the other side. Both sides should be well browned.

This is nice as a treat for children (and adults). My dad often liked to end his evening meal with a sweet paratha.

Puris (Deep fried bread)

Puris are quicker to make than rotis and parathas. The best puris are those that puff-up into a ball when fried. It takes some practice to achieve this. However, the following have to be ensured to get a satisfactory result:

- the dough has to be slightly harder than roti dough.

- oil has to be the right temperature before starting the frying process (to make sure that the oil is hot enough for the puris to fry, drop a pinch of dough in it – if it immediately sizzles to the top then the oil is ready).

- rolling has to be so that the puris are thicker at the centre and thinner at the edge

- have someone help you either fry or roll (if managing alone, best is to roll out all the puris first – if more than 20, do it in batches)

Puris taste fantastic when served hot with their puffiness still intact. They are very nice for picnics, and for children's as well as other parties. In fact, children love making them. My grandson, Gethin, by the age of eight was able to make the dough and roll out the puris perfectly. I simply did the frying part.
As they are deep fried, puris can stay for a week or so in the fridge.

PLAIN PURIS

Cooking time:
15 - 20 minutes

1 cup flour
just under ½ cup water
1 ½ tablespoons oil

OIL FOR FRYING

Mix flour with oil and small amounts of water at a time and knead dough which is slightly harder than roti dough (dough can be made well in advance). Divide it in 16 balls.

Place a small wok on heat with enough oil to deep fry 16 puris. Touch the ball of dough with a drop of oil and roll into thin round shape (approximately ½ mm thick).

Carefully drop it in hot oil and gently press its centre with a chalani (spatula) – this helps the puri puff-up. Turn over within 20 seconds. Give the other side 20 seconds also. Take it out draining as much oil as possible.

Puri made with plain flour is called Luchi in Bengal

SPICY PURIS

Cooking time:
15 - 20 minutes

1 cup flour
just under ½ cup water
1 tablespoon oil
½ teaspoon salt
½ teaspoon chili powder (optional)
½ teaspoon of ajwain or oregano
½ teaspoon of turmeric (optional)

OIL FOR FRYING

Mix flour with 1 spoon of oil, other ingredients and small amounts of water at a time and knead dough which is slightly harder than roti dough (dough can be made well in advance).Divide it in 16 balls.

Place a small wok on heat with enough oil to deep fry 16 puris. Touch the ball of dough with drop of oil and roll into thin round shape (approximately ½ mm thick).

Carefully drop it in hot oil and gently press its centre with a chalani (spatula) – this helps the puri puff up. Turn over within 20 seconds. Give the other side 20 seconds also. Take it out draining as much oil as possible.

This makes a very tempting afternoon snack, especially on a rainy day

KACHORI (Dal Puri)

Cooking time:
40 minutes

1 cup flour
under ½ cup water
1 tablespoon oil
½ teaspoon salt

Filling

½ cup urad dal
(washed and soaked for an hour at least)
1 green or red chilli
1 inch piece of ginger

OIL FOR FRYING

Drain all the water from dal, place dal and all other filling ingredients in grinder and grind into a rough dough.

Mix flour with oil and small amounts of water at a time and knead dough which is slightly harder than roti dough (dough can be made well in advance).

Divide the dough and the filling into 16 balls each.

Place small wok on heat with enough oil to deep fry 16 kachoris. Touch the ball of dough with drop of oil and roll into thick round shape. Place the filling in the middle and bring the edges together and squeeze at the top. Using a drop of oil on the ball, gently roll out into round kachori.

Carefully drop it in hot oil and gently press its centre with a chalani (spatula). Turn over within 20 seconds. Give the other side 20 seconds also. Take it out draining as much oil as possible.

This goes best with potatoes in gravy and sweet and sour pumpkin.

BHATURA

Cooking time:
15 - 20 minutes

1 cup plain flour
3 table spoons sour yoghurt
1 tablespoon oil
½ teaspoon baking powder
½ teaspoon salt
¼ teaspoon sugar
¼ cup water

OIL FOR FRYING

Mix flour with all ingredients and small amounts of water at a time and knead dough which is slightly harder than roti dough.

Place the dough in large bowl, cover with a damp napkin and leave it in a warm place for 2 to 3 hours. Knead the dough again and divide it in 12 balls.

Place small wok on heat with enough oil to deep fry 12 bhaturas. Touch the ball of dough with drop of oil and roll into thin round shape (approximately 1mm thick).

Carefully drop it in hot oil and gently press its centre with a chalani (spatula). Turn over within 20 seconds. Give the other side 20 seconds also. Take it out draining as much oil as possible.

This is best served with cholle.

Salads
&Raitas

In my experience the most appropriate salad with hot and spicy food is a simple one – tomatoes, cucumber, beetroot, onions, lettuce etc. chopped fresh (in desired combination) and sprinkled with a touch of lemon juice. A side salad is almost a must to balance an Indian meal. It provides the fresh crunchy touch to the meal and additional essential vitamins and minerals to the persons eating. Salads can be simple ones with just a touch of lemon or elaborate ones with hot garnish. But when deciding which one, ensure that your choice complements the meal.

SAMBHARO (Gujarati)

½ cup finely chopped cabbage
¼ cup finely chopped carrots (thin and long)
¼ cup finely chopped cucumber (thin and long)
2 green chillies – split in half, length ways
2-3 tablespoon lemon juice
½ teaspoon sugar
½ teaspoon salt
pinch of turmeric powder

Baghaar

1 tablespoon oil
1 teaspoon mustard seeds
¼ teaspoon asafoetida
6 curry leaves

Mix all the main ingredients together.

In a frying pan heat oil and put in the mustard seeds. When they pop, put in asafoetida and curry leaves. Turn the heat off and add the main ingredients. Toss well and serve.

This can be prepared in advance and warmed up for 15 seconds in microwave or by a quick toss on very high temp so that the vegetables do not lose water.

MIXED SALAD

1 small tomato (sliced thin and round)
5cm piece of cucumber (sliced thin and round)
1 small onion (sliced thin and round)
2 leaves of crunchy lettuce (chopped into fine shreds)
2 - 3 tablespoons of lemon juice

Before serving mix in 2 - 4 table spoons of lemon juice.

KOSHAMBIR (Maharashtran)

1 medium tomato
1 medium onion
5cm cucumber
½ green chilli (chopped very fine)
¼ cup green coriander leaves (chopped)
2-3 tablespoons lemon juice
1 tablespoon roasted peanuts (crushed)
1 tablespoon desiccated coconut
½ teaspoon sugar
½ teaspoon salt

Dice all the vegetables into small cubes and mix in all other ingredients.

Best with plain food

CABBAGE SALAD (Kerala)

¼ kg of cabbage shredded finely
2 green chillies split in 2 (lengthways)
½ teaspoon salt
6 tablespoons of shredded coconut,
½ cup green coriander leaves (chopped fine)
2-3 tablespoons of lemon juice.

Mix all ingredients and serve.

BEETROOT (Kerala)

1 large beetroot
(boiled, peeled and diced into small cubes)
1 green chilli chopped in small pieces
2-3 tablespoons of lemon juice.
½ teaspoon salt

Baghaar

1 teaspoon oil
1 teaspoon mustard seeds
1 pod garlic – finely chopped
4 curry leaves
1 tablespoon sesame seeds
OR 1 tablespoon shredded coconut,

In a frying pan heat oil. Put in the mustard seeds. When they pop, put in all other baghaar items and turn the heat off. Mix in the main ingredients. Toss well and serve.

This can be prepared in advance and be served hot or cold

MULI (white raddish) SALAD (Cooked)

¼ kg of muli (grated)
2 green chillies split in 2 (lengthways)
½ teaspoon salt
2-3 tablespoons of lemon juice.
pinch of turmeric

Baghaar

1 tablespoon oil (if possible mustard oil)
½ teaspoon mustard seeds
pinch asafoetida

Heat oil in a wok, or a wide pan. Pop the mustard seeds and add asafoetida. Mix in all the main ingredients and toss once and turn off the heat. Serve hot or cold.

MULI SALAD

¼ kg of muli - grated
2 green chilies split in 2 (lengthways)
3cm of ginger chopped fine
½ teaspoon salt
2 - 3 tablespoons of lemon juice.
¼ cup green coriander leaves
OR mint leaves (chopped)

Mix all the salad ingredients and serve.

FRUIT SALAD

1 apple or guava
1 banana
5cm of cucumber
1 small capsicum
1 mango (if in season)
(all chopped into medium size cubes)
2 - 4 table spoons lemon juice
1 teaspoon roasted and crushed cumin seeds *
¼ teaspoon finely ground black pepper *
¼ teaspoon finely ground ginger *
pinch of red chilli powder *
¼ teaspoon nutmeg powder *
¾ teaspoon salt *
¼ cup green mint (chopped)

* OR use 2-3 table spoons of ready made Chatt Masala
instead of these ingredients

Toss all ingredients together and serve.

This can also be served as a starter.

CARROT SALAD

1 large carrot (grated)
2 tablespoons of roasted peanuts (roughly crushed)
2 tablespoons of sultana
½ teaspoon salt
1 finely chopped green chilli (optional)
2-4 tablespoons of lemon juice.
¼ cup green coriander leaves (chopped)

Toss all ingredients together and servet

CARROT AND CUCUMBER SALAD

1 small carrot (grated)
2 inch cucumber (grated)
¼ cup fresh coriander (chopped)
½ teaspoon salt
1 finely chopped green chilli (optional)
2-4 tablespoons of lemon juice.

Toss all ingredients together and serve

TOMATO SALAD

2 medium tomatoes - sliced into thin rounds
1 small onion - sliced into very thin rounds
½ teaspoon salt
¼ teaspoon sugar
2 tablespoons of lemon juice or vinegar
¼ cup green coriander leaves (chopped)
1 finely chopped green chilli (optional)

Soak the onion rings in lemon/vinegar, sugar and salt for at least ½ hour.

Toss all ingredients together and serve

Raita

Raita is a mixture of yoghurt and raw or cooked vegetable. It can also be made with fruits and something called Bundi. Bundi (droplets) are tiny deep fried balls (smaller than peas) prepared from gram flour. They are cumbersome to make so are best bought ready-made.

The best yoghurt for raitas is live, thick, preferably Greek style yoghurt. A small amount of crushed mustard seeds are added to most raitas. These can be crushed and kept for 'as and when' use. But bottled granulated mustard works equally well.

Raita adds a cooling element to the meal and also contributes towards making a meal nutritionally balanced.

Raitas can also be used as dips with starters and munchies such as crisps and tortillas.

CUCUMBER RAITA (most cooling of all)

1 cup yoghurt
¼ cup grated cucumber
¼ teaspoon salt
¼ teaspoon sugar
¼ teaspoon mustard seeds (ground rough)

Garnish

¼ cup green coriander leaves (chopped)
OR mint

Mix all the main ingredients together and decorate with coriander/mint.

BANANA RAITA

1 cup yoghurt
1 small ripe banana (chopped into rings or small pieces)
¼ teaspoon salt
¼ teaspoon mustard seeds (ground rough)

Garnish

¼ cup green coriander leaves (chopped)

Mix all the main ingredients together and decorate with coriander

MIXED SALAD RAITA

1 cup yoghurt
1 small tomato
1 small onion
2cm cucumber
¼ teaspoon salt
¼ teaspoon sugar
1 tablespoon roasted peanuts crushed (optional)

Garnish

¼ cup green coriander leaves
OR mint (chopped)

Mix all the main ingredients together and decorate with coriander/mint.

PUMPKIN / CARROT RAITA

1 cup yoghurt
1 medium carrot
OR carrot size piece of pumpkin
(boiled and mashed)
¼ teaspoon salt
¼ teaspoon sugar

Baghaar

1 teaspoon oil
¼ teaspoon cumin seeds
¼ teaspoon fenugreek seeds
¼ teaspoon asafoetida
1 whole dried red chilli

Mix all the main ingredients together. Heat oil in a small bowl, add cumin, fenugreek asafoedita and chilli.

When brown pour on top of raita.

BUNDI RAITA 1

1 cup yoghurt
¼ cup bundi
¼ to ½ cup water
OR milk
¼ teaspoon salt
¼ teaspoon sugar

Garnish

1 tea spoon roasted cumin seeds (crushed)

Mix all the main ingredients together, sprinkle cumin and serve.

BUNDI RAITA 2

1 cup yoghurt
¼ cup bundi
¼ to ½ cup water
OR milk
¼ teaspoon salt
1 tablespoon sweet mint chutney (pg 243)

Mix all the ingredients together and serve

LAUKI / MARROW RAITA

1 cup yoghurt
¼ cup lauki or marrow (grated)
¼ teaspoon salt

Baghaar

1 teaspoon oil
¼ teaspoon cumin seeds
¼ teaspoon asafoetida
1 whole dried red chilli

On gentle heat cook the lauki/marrow in its own water till tender (4-5 minutes). When it cools mix all the main ingredients together.

Heat oil in a small bowl, add cumin, asafoetida and chilli. When brown pour on top of raita.

AUBERGINE RAITA 1

1 cup yoghurt
1 small or ¼ kg aubergine
¼ teaspoon salt
¼ teaspoon garlic (paste)
¼ cup green coriander leaves chopped

Garnish

1 teaspoon mustard oil
¼ teaspoon cumin seeds (roasted and crushed)
¼ teaspoon chilli powder

Roast the aubergine whole in a hot oven or under the grill (make sure to pierce in one or two places). When cold remove the charred skin and mash. Mix all the main ingredients together. Spread oil on top and sprinkle cumin and chilli.

This can also be made by mixing in ½ tablespoon of roasted sesame seeds and ½ tablespoon of roasted peanuts (crushed).

AUBERGINE RAITA 2

1 cup yoghurt
1 small or ¼ kg aubergine
¼ teaspoon salt
¼ teaspoon garam masala
¼ teaspoon chilli powder
¼ cup green mint (chopped)

OIL FOR FRYING

Baghaar

2 tablespoons of oil
¼ teaspoon cumin seeds
¼ teaspoon garlic (paste)
¼ teaspoon ginger (paste)

Chop the aubergine into cubes and deep fry the pieces. When cold mix the aubergine pieces and all the other main ingredients in the yoghurt, taking care that the pieces do not mush up.

Heat oil in a small bowl, add cumin seeds and when they brown stir in ginger and garlic paste. Take the mix off the heat and pour on top of raita.

Chutneys
& Pickles

Chutneys and pickles not only add that extra zest to a meal but also help complete the six distinct tastes defined in Ayurveda and in general complement the dishes of a given menu. Moreover, chutneys are an essential accompaniment for most of the Indian snacks, especially pakoras.

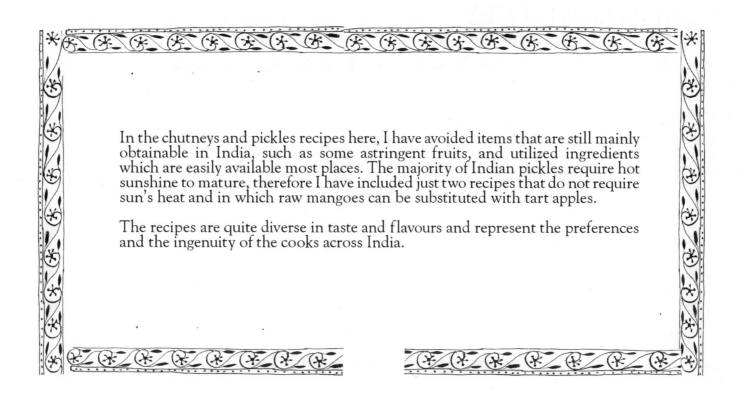

In the chutneys and pickles recipes here, I have avoided items that are still mainly obtainable in India, such as some astringent fruits, and utilized ingredients which are easily available most places. The majority of Indian pickles require hot sunshine to mature, therefore I have included just two recipes that do not require sun's heat and in which raw mangoes can be substituted with tart apples.

The recipes are quite diverse in taste and flavours and represent the preferences and the ingenuity of the cooks across India.

MIX SALAD CHUTNEY

2cm piece of cucumber
½ small carrot
½ small capsicum
1 large pod garlic
1 green chilli
¼ cup green coriander leaves or mint
¾ teaspoon salt
½ teaspoon cumin seeds or powder
2 - 3 tablespoons of tamarind pulp
¼ cup of water

Chop all ingredients roughly and blend them into a fine paste.

Best with crispy potato pokaras.

CORIANDER (Hot)

2 cup green coriander leaves
2 green chillies
½ teaspoon salt
2 pods garlic

Put all ingredients in blender and blend to a fine paste.

Best for bhel or as an accompaniment with mild food

MINT OR CORIANDER (Sweet)

3 cups fresh mint
OR green coriander leaves
1 green chilli
¾ teaspoon salt
3 - 4 tablespoons sugar
4 - 6 tablespoons lemon juice
(can be substituted with 1 small raw mango - peeled and chopped)
1 teaspoon cumin seeds
¼ teaspoon asafoetida

Put all ingredients in blender and blend to a fine paste.

Best with any pakora or chillas.

MINT OR CORIANDER (Sour)

2 cups fresh mint
OR green coriander leaves
1 green chilli
¾ teaspoon salt
1 medium onion chopped
4 - 6 tablespoons lemon juice
(can be substituted with vinegar or raw mango)
1 teaspoon cumin seeds

Put all ingredients in blender and blend to a fine paste.

Best with any pakora or chillas

MANGO OR COOKING APPLE OR GOOSEBERRY OR PLUM

1 large raw mango/ cooking apple (peeled and chopped)
OR 1 cup gooseberries/ stoned plums
2 tablespoons oil
¼ teaspoon fenugreek seeds
¼ teaspoon cumin seeds
¼ teaspoon asafoetida
½ teaspoon crushed chilli
¼ teaspoon turmeric
¾ teaspoon salt
4 - 6 tablespoons sugar
2 pods of crushed garlic (optional)

Heat oil in a pan, add fenugreek, cumin and asafoetida. When brown (add garlic and brown it) add mango or fruit of choice. Mix in other ingredients and cook on gentle heat until soft and mushy. Serve cold. The chutney should be on the sweet side – add extra sugar if needed.

This can be made in larger quantity and bottled by adding vinegar (2 table spoons for above amount) and extra sugar and salt.

This can be made by adding a few pieces of cinnamon sticks

COCONUT 1

1 cup shredded coconut
1 whole red chillis (medium)
¾ teaspoon salt
1 pods of garlic
2 - 3 tablespoon tamarind juice (thick)

Roast coconut, chilli, garlic separately
Put all ingredients in blender and blend to a rough consistency

Best as an accompaniment with mild food or as a sandwich filling

COCONUT 2

½ cup shredded coconut
1 cup yogurt
1 green chilli (medium)
¾ teaspoon salt
1 - 2 table spoons sugar

Baghaar

1 tablespoon oil
½ teaspoon mustard seeds
¼ teaspoon asafoetida
6 curry leaves
1 whole red chilli

Blend the main ingredients in a blender.

Heat oil in a small pan and add mustard seeds and when they pop add asafoetida, red chilli and curry leaves. Pour it over the coconut blend.

Same can be made with fresh mint – add a handful of leaves at the blending stage.

Best with handovo and pakoras

COCONUT 3

1 cup shredded coconut
1 green chilli
¼ cup tender curry leaves
2 tablespoons of roasted gram or peanuts
¾ teaspoon salt
3 - 4 tablespoons lemon juice

Baghaar

½ tablespoon oil
½ teaspoon mustard seeds
¼ teaspoon asafoetida
1 whole red chilli

Blend the main ingredients in a blender.

Heat oil in a small pan and add mustard seeds and when they pop add asafoetida, red chilli and curry leaves. Pour it over the coconut blend.

Best with South Indian dishes such as dosa/idli.

TOMATO

4 tomatoes (medium)
1 green chilli (chopped fine)
½ teaspoon salt
1 pod garlic (optional) (roasted and crushed)
1 teaspoon cumin seeds (roasted and crushed)
¼ cup green mint
OR green coriander leaves (chopped)
2 tablespoons mustard
OR olive oil

Roast whole tomatoes under a grill until their skin is charred. When cold remove the skin and squash the tomatoes well. Mix into the tomato all the ingredients and serve.

Good as a side dish or accompaniment for pakoras

TOMATO (Sweet)

4 medium tomatoes (finely chopped)
1 green chilli (chopped)
¼ teaspoon turmeric
¾ teaspoon salt
1 - 2 tablespoons sugar
1 tablespoon of ginger (finely chopped)

For Baghaar

1 tablespoon oil
½ teaspoon fenugreek seeds
½ teaspoon cumin seeds
¼ teaspoon asafoetida

Heat oil in a pan and add fenugreek, cumin. When they pop add asafoetida. When brown add the tomatoes and all other ingredients. Cook on gentle heat for 10 minutes. Serve hot or cold.

Good as a side dish with mild food

SWEET TAMARIND

1 cup tamarind pulp
1 teaspoon crushed chilli
1 - 1 ½ teaspoon salt
6 - 8 tablespoons sugar
1 teaspoon cumin seeds (roasted and crushed)
1 pod garlic finely chopped (optional)

Blend all ingredients together. This is a sweet chutney, therefore add more sugar if needed.

FENUGREEK & GINGER RELISH

¼ cup fenugreek seeds (soaked for at least 2 hours)
¼ cup ginger chopped fine
1 small tomato (chopped)
¼ teaspoon salt
pinch of chilli powder

Baghaar

1 teaspoon oil
¼ teaspoon asafoetida

In a pan heat the oil and add asafoetida. When it bubbles mix in all other ingredients and cook on gentle heat for 5 minutes.

Serve hot or cold.

This is a bitter sweet relish which adds that extra savour to a meal and can be served as a main or a side dish.

RAW MANGO/ APPLE PICKLE (Sweet)

4 medium mangoes/ tart apples
1 ½ teaspoon salt
16 - 18 tablespoons sugar
1 teaspoon crushed chilli
1 teaspoon cumin seeds
½ teaspoon asafoetida

Peel the mangoes/apples and grate them (thick). Mix the salt and fruit and sit for an hour. Squeeze all the juice out of the fruit. Place the juice, sugar, chilli, cumin seeds and asafoetida in a pot and cook them on low heat till it thickens to a syrup. Add the fruit and cook for few more minutes. When cold store in air-tight jar.

This will keep for months.

RAW MANGO/ APPLE PICKLE (Hot)

3 medium mangoes/ tart apples
2 teaspoons of salt
1 teaspoon crushed chilli
1 tablespoon fennel seeds
1 tablespoon fenugreek seeds
1 teaspoon mustard seeds
½ teaspoon kalonji (nigella sativa)
½ teaspoon asafoetida
½ teaspoon turmeric
1 cup oil (preferably mustard oil)

Cut the fruit into bite size pieces, mix in turmeric and half the salt. Arrange the mixture on one side of a tray and place the tray tilted with the fruit sitting on the raised part. Leave it for 6-7 hours for the fruit to release juices. Throw away the juice and dab the fruit dry with a clean cloth or tissues.

Heat oil in a pan and take off the heat. Mix in all the ingredients (except the fruit) in hot oil. After a few minutes mix in the fruit. When the mixture is absolutely cold store it in air-tight jar. For a few days, now and again, stir the pickle and ensure all the fruit is well coated with oil.

This will keep for months.

Drinks
& Sweets

Drinks

Generally, water is what most Indians would drink with their meals. However, a yoghurt drink with salt (lassi, mattha) is often served with meals particularly in summer as, besides its many properties, yoghurt has also a cooling effect on the body. Wine and beer indeed add to the pleasure of Indian food, especially the richer variety.

Sweet lassi/milkshakes are in-between-meals drinks. The best sweet lassi, as far as I am concerned, is still served in Mumbai from a little outlet in Dadar area. The café has been there for at least fifty years with hardly any changes in ambience or the quality of food and drinks. The lassi is made with fresh yoghurt and is served with a thick layer of skin (malai) which forms on the top when yoghurt sets, and that's what makes it irresistible.

Of course, there is also chai (tea). Chai is something most Indians can drink anytime (especially my mother – she needs at least two cups of stronger than strong chai before she can start her day). Chai, like Indian food, varies from region to region. For instance, in the mountain regions of the north, black sweet tea is imbibed with a spoonful of butter to fortify the self against severe winter weather. Some prefer the tea brewed in a teapot with milk and sugar added according to taste and others would not call this tea. For them a strong, sugary, boiled concoction which is a mixture of milk, water, sugar, and tea leaves, bubbled in a pot to a particular strength, is real tea or chai. Depending on the taste, region and season, crushed or whole spice of preference (or those that help fight off colds, coughs, and fever) such as ginger, cardamom, clove, nutmeg, cinnamon, basil, mint - or a powdered mixture of all these called chai masala - is often added to this brew to give it that extra boost. Tea with chai masala (even the tea bag kind) works wonders in winter – one can feel the warmth surging through the body with every sip. Chai, like espresso coffee, has a real kick to it and, like espresso, is mostly drunk from small cups.

CHAI

4 cups of a half and half mix of milk and water
1 tea bag or teaspoon of loose tea (strong variety) per cup

Sugar according to taste
¼ teaspoon per cup of spice according to preference

In a pot, bring the liquid to boil with all other ingredients in it. Leave the mixture to simmer for 2 to 3 minutes. Strain and serve.

SWEET LASSI

500g tub of yoghurt - preferably Greek style
8 teaspoons of sugar (vary this according to taste)
finely crushed seeds of 1 cardamom (optional)
½ litre of water
16 to 20 ice cubes

Put all ingredients (except the ice cubes) in a liquidizer and whisk for 2 to 3 minutes OR put the ingredients in a pot and, using an electric or hand blender, whisk till nicely frothy. Place 4 to 5 ice cubes in each glass, pour the lassi and serve.

As a decoration, a pinch of pistachio powder can be sprinkled on top.

MANGO LASSI

As above BUT when blending also add either slices of 1 ripe mango OR ½ cup of mango pulp

SALT LASSI

500g of yoghurt - preferably Greek style
½ teaspoon of salt (vary this according to taste)
1 teaspoon of roasted cumin seeds (finely crushed)
1/2 litre of water
16 to 20 ice cubes (optional)

Put all the ingredients in a liquidizer and whisk for 2 to 3 minutes OR put the ingredients in a pot and, using an electric or hand blender, whisk till frothy. Place 4 to 5 ice cubes in each glass, pour the lassi and serve.

As a decoration a few mint or coriander leaves can be placed on top.

SALT LASSI 2 (with mint)

As above BUT when blending also add either 1 tablespoon of sweet mint chutney or a few mint leaves and ½ teaspoon of sugar

MATTHA 1

250g tub of yoghurt - preferably Greek style
½ teaspoon of salt (vary this according to taste)
1 teaspoon of roasted cumin seeds (finely crushed)
½ litre of water

MATTHA 2

Blend as in mattha 1, BUT without the cumin. Instead do a baghaar with ½ teaspoon of cumin seeds and ½ teaspoon of asafoetida roasted in 1 teaspoon of oil.

MATTHA 3

Blend as in mattha 1 BUT without the cumin. Instead do a baghaar with ½ teaspoon of mustard seeds, ½ teaspoon of asafoetida and 4 curry leaves roasted in 1 teaspoon of oil.

MATTHA 4

All as in mattha 1 BUT when blending also add either 1 tablespoon of sweet mint chutney or a few mint leaves and ½ teaspoon of sugar.

(Mattha is a thinner version of salt lassi)

Put all the ingredients in a liquidizer and whisk for 2 to 3 minutes OR put the ingredients in a pot and, using an electric or hand blender, whisk till frothy and serve.

MANGO MILK SHAKE

Slices of 2 ripe mangoes
OR 1 cup of mango pulp
1 litre of full cream milk
6 teaspoons of sugar (vary according to taste)
16 - 20 ice cubes

Put all ingredients (except the ice cubes) into a liquidizer and whisk for 2 - 3 minutes or put the ingredients in a pot and, using an electric or hand blender, whisk till nicely frothy. Place 4 - 5 ice cubes in each glass, pour the milkshake and serve.

As a decoration pinch of almonds or pistachio powder can be sprinkled on top.

This drink can be made with:
½ cup of very finely ground almonds and ½ teaspoon of cardamom powder.

Children love milkshakes and made with fruit or almonds they are temptingly tasty as well as nourishing.

Sweets

Growing up in India, sweets and puddings were items that, in my family, were generally dished out during festivals, weddings and other special occasions. Our dessert was either fresh fruits or a mixture of nuts and sultanas which my naniji would give out after lunch. We happily munched these away without a care for other type of sweets. Yet, the variety of sweets produced in India is not only endless but also very inspired. Indian sweets and puddings are made from every possible ingredient including fruits, vegetables, lentils, rice and – my most favourite – milk and milk products. **However, you will note that very few Indian sweets are made with wheat flour.** In this section I have charted out just a few recipes - some easy to make and some not so simple.

When making these sweets it is best to:

- Use a heavy base pot or pan – these are not only better in terms of heat efficiency but also don't easily burn the food.

CARROT HALVA

3 good size carrots – approximately 500g (scraped and washed)
1½ litres of milk
OR ½ litre of milk and 1 tin (170g) of evaporated milk
crushed seeds of 4 cardamoms
½ cup of thinly chopped almonds and pistachio nuts
½ cup of ghee or unsalted butter (approximately 175g)
¾ cup of sugar

Grate the carrots and put them in a large pot. Add the milk and place it on a high heat. Occasionally stir the mixture and make sure it is not catching at the bottom of the pot. Once it comes to the boil, lower the heat to medium and let it cook (with occasional stirring) until the milk has thickened.

Add the nuts, cardamom and evaporated milk (if using it). Let the mixture dry out some more and then add ghee/butter. Keep cooking and stirring (more often at this stage) till it is dryish. Add the sugar and continue to stir till the liquid has evaporated and the ghee starts to show.

This sweet can be served hot or cold (room temperature). I prefer it cold by itself but it can be served hot with ice-cream or cream. While I make this sweet dry (but moist) it can also be made slightly soggy.

This is a laborious and time-consuming dish to make. But once done it can be kept for days in the fridge or for longer in the freezer. Therefore, I have given measurements which will give 8 or more helpings. This is a first-rate nourishing pudding for winter.

KHEER (Rice Pudding)

2 tablespoons of rice (washed)
1½ litres of milk or 1 litre of milk and 1 tin (170g) of evaporated milk
crushed seeds of 2 cardamoms
¼ cup of thinly chopped almonds and/or pistachio nuts
¼ cup of sugar (vary according to taste)

In a large pan, bring the milk to the boil. Lower the heat and let the milk simmer till it has halved in quantity. Occasionally stir the milk and make sure it is not burning at the bottom of the pot. Add the rice and cook for about 10 minutes on a low heat.

Add the sugar, cardamom, nuts and evaporated milk, (if using it). Simmer the mixture for another 10 minutes and serve (hot or cold).

Kheer should be of a thick soup consistency.

KHEER WITH MANGO

Cook the kheer as above.
When completely cold, add cubed pieces of 1 ripe mango. Serve cold.

This sweet can also be made with:
2 grated apples
OR with segments of 2 satsumas.

SHRIKHAND

2 cups of curd cheese
½ cup of milk (less or more according to the requirement)
1¼ cups of sugar (vary according to taste)
½ teaspoon of saffron
OR crushed cardamom seeds
2 tablespoons of finely chopped almonds
OR pistachio
OR a mixture of both

Whisk the curd cheese, sugar and saffron together. Gradually whisk in the milk till the mixture is smooth and the consistency of a thick custard. Put the mixture in a serving dish, sprinkle the nuts and leave it in the fridge for at least 2 hours. Serve cold.

This sweet can be made with:

1) ½ cup of diced fruits - mangoes and oranges or other fruits of choice - can be mixed in the shrikhand just before sprinkling the nuts.

2) ½ cup of mango slices can be blended in at the whisking stage, making it a mango flavoured shrikhand.

SEMOLINA HALVA

¾ cup coarse semolina
2 tablespoons of ghee
OR unsalted butter
3 cups of milk or water
½ cup of sugar (vary according to taste)
½ teaspoon of crushed cardamom seeds
2 tablespoons of finely chopped almonds

In a wok, heat the ghee and add the semolina. Lower the heat and gently roast till the semolina is nicely browned (if using butter, dry roast the semolina on low heat, when browned, mix in butter). Add milk/water and bring to the boil, cook for a minute or so and add the sugar and nuts. Stir till the mixture is dry but moist. Serve hot or cold.

To make a richer halva, use 1 cup of milk and ½ cup of evaporated milk.

This can also be served a bit runny (thick soup consistency) by adding extra milk (and if required, also extra sugar).

I don't know why but in India, halva seems to be part of the menu for all auspicious occasions for Hindus. Most people, when making this halva, boil the mix of water and sugar separately and then add it to the browned semolina. I find my method equally effective and also more time and resource efficient.

SEMOLINA HALVA 2

½ cup of coarse semolina
2 tablespoons of ghee
OR unsalted butter
2 cups of milk
¼ cup of sugar
½ teaspoon of crushed cardamom seeds
150g (half packet) of marzipan

In a wok, heat the ghee and add the semolina. Lower the heat and gently roast till the semolina is nicely browned (if using butter, dry roast the semolina on low heat, when browned, mix in the butter). Add milk, sugar and crumble in the marzipan. Bring to the boil and cook on a low heat till the mixture is dry but moist. Serve hot or cold.

My younger sister has invented this version of semolina halva which is not only delicious but also easier to make.

VERMICELLI (Dry)

1 cup of the thinnest vermicelli
1½ cups of water
just over ½ cup of sugar (vary according to taste)
½ teaspoon of crushed cardamom seeds or 4 spoons rose water
2 tablespoons of finely chopped almonds
1 tablespoon of ghee or unsalted butter

In a wok, heat the ghee and add the vermicelli, lower the heat and gently roast till the vermicelli is nicely browned. Boil the water separately and add to the vermicelli. Bring the mix to the boil and cook for a minute or so. Add the sugar and nuts and stir till the mixture is dry but moist. Add cardamom/rose water and serve hot or cold.

Our Muslim neighbours in Mumbai (as well as in London), along with other goodies, always treated us to this aromatic delicacy on Eid day – and what a treat!

Also try this steaming hot, with a dollop of thick creamy yoghurt on top – it's too delicious for words. This was served for breakfast at my Irani friend's wedding. I gather it is an Iranian custom for such occasions. I enjoyed the dish so much that I have never bothered to wait for another Irani wedding - I just prepare it when I like.

VERMICELLI PUDDING

For a variation to the above recipe, use ½ cup of vermicelli, ½ spoon of ghee AND instead of water mix in 2 cups of milk and ½ cup of evaporated milk. Boil this for a few minutes (consistency of thick soup) and serve hot or cold.

Malai

Malai is the skin that forms on milk when it is heated.

Rabdi

is layer upon layer of this skin, sweetened, and eaten by itself or with other things such as puris, parathas. It can also be used in making other sweets such as rasmali, barfi etc.

Method for Rabdi

- In a large frying pan bring to boil a litre of full cream milk and then leave it to simmer, stirring from time to time to ensure that the milk does not catch at the bottom. Gently move each layer of malai to one side so that another layer can form. Continue this till the liquid is reduced to soft malai.

Mawa

Make rabdi as above. Continue to stir more frequently till rabdi has turned into a dry lump. Two litres of full cream milk will give you approximately one cup of mawa.

RABDI DESSERT

Make rabdi with 1 litre of milk. Turn off the heat and add sugar according to taste. When the rabdi is cold mix in two spoons of rose or kaveda water (optional). Serve at room temperature on its own or with fruits.

RABDI WITH PANCAKE

You can use ready made pancakes or make fresh ones.

Place 1-2 table spoons of rabdi on each pancake, roll the pancake and place it on a serving dish. Serve with slices or cubes of fresh mango and a sprig of mint.

BARFI (PLAIN)

2 cups full cream milk powder or 1 cup mawa (pg. 264)
½ cup milk (reduce this to few spoons if using mawa)
just over ¾ cup sugar (vary according to taste)
½ teaspoon crushed cardamom seeds
½ cup ghee or unsalted butter
(reduce this to 1 spoon if using mawa)

In a large pan heat the ghee, milk and sugar. Gently bring it to boil. Add milk powder and cook for 10 - 12 minutes (for mawa reduce this time to 5 mins) on low heat, stirring frequently. Mix in the cardamom. Transfer to a well buttered dish. When cool cut into small pieces

OTHER BARFI

Add ½ cup of finely chopped almonds
OR pistachio nuts
OR desiccated coconut
AND ¼ cup extra sugar before adding
milk powder/mawa to the ghee mix.

GRAM FLOUR PANJEERI

3 cups gram flour (approx 300 grams)
200 grams butter (unsalted) or ghee
450 grams tin condensed milk (sweet)
½ teaspoon of crushed cardamom seeds
20 almonds (finely chopped)

Grease a 10 inch shallow dish with a tea spoon of butter. Melt rest of the butter in a large thick bottom pan and stir in the gram flour. Cook on very gentle heat till the flour is nicely browned.

In another pan bring to boil the condensed milk (again use a thick pan so it doesn't catch at the bottom). Add cardamom and pour the boiling liquid into the still hot gram flour. Mix it well together and evenly spread the mixture in the greased dish.

Sprinkle the almonds and pat them down gently. When cool cut into desired size pieces.

This will keep for at least a week and longer in the fridge (can be frozen as well).

This is one of my experiments which has worked really well.

DATE AND NUT ROLL 1

2 cups de-stoned dates
OR 1 cup of each - figs and dates
½ cup mixed nuts (almonds/cashews/hazelnuts etc.)
2 table spoons water

Roast the nuts and grind them rough (crumbly). Place the water in a shallow pan and heat it. Add dates, mix and turn the heat off (or microwave dates sprinkled with water for a minute).

While still hot mush the dates to a paste. Add the nuts and mix well together. Shape the mixture into a thick roll. Cut to desired size pieces.

This can keep for days.

This is a very healthy, very tasty snack for children and adults as it does not require any butter/ghee or cooking. This is one of the few sweets Rahul, my son, (who is now a vegan and into healthy food) can enjoy without any qualms. Credit for the recipe goes to my friend Asha from Southall. Asha has been my friend ever since I first arrived in London. Over the last 40 years her family have treated me as one of their own and I have learnt from her and her mum to cook some wholesome Gujarati food.

DATE AND NUT ROLL 2

1 cup de-stoned dates
OR ½ cup of each - figs and dates
1 cup oat flakes
½ cup mixed nuts (almonds/cashews/hazelnuts etc.)
2 table spoons water

Dry roast the nuts and grind them rough (crumbly). Dry roast the oats in a frying pan. Place the water in a shallow pan and heat it. Add dates, mix and turn the heat off (or microwave dates sprinkled with water for a minute).

While still hot, mush the dates to a paste. Add the nuts and oats and mix well together. Shape the mixture into a thick roll. Cut to desired size pieces.

This can keep for days

To Rahul's delight I have added yet another extremely healthy ingredient to Asha's recipe with an appetizing result. The roasted oats give the roll an extra flavour and crunch.

KULFI (Plain)

soft malai made with 1 litre full cream milk (pg 264)
400 gram tin evaporated milk
½ cup sugar
½ teaspoon crushed cardamom
OR saffron

Whip the evaporated milk and sugar into a frothy mix. Gently blend in the malai and cardamom. Pour the mixture in a tub and place in the freezer for at least 8 hours. Serve cut into bite size cubes.

Kulfi is simply a richer version of ice cream with a distinct flavour and texture. It makes a perfect dessert by itself or with other complementary western or eastern puddings.

OTHER KULFI

To the above:

Add ¼ cup extra sugar at the whipping point AND with the malai also blend in
1 cup mashed up mango
OR ½ cup of finely chopped almonds
OR ½ cup of finely chopped pistachio nuts.

Planning A Meal

The importance of selecting your dishes for each meal cannot be over estimated. To get the best from each meal they have to be thought through and planned according to the time of day, season and reason (e.g. festival, party), nutritional balance and the preferences of your family or guests. Crucial to the success is also the time element – ensure that you have sufficient time to prepare the dishes you have planned. If not, change the menu to suit the time available to you.

When it comes to food I am a highly organised person. My daily meals are worked out with a view to variety (different lentils, seasonal vegetables), nutrition and taste. Mostly I alternate between plain and spicy, North Indian and non-North Indian meals. For example, if on Monday I have cooked plain moong dal (pg 92), cauliflower with potatoes (pg 137), to go with rice and roti, served with a simple salad and plain yoghurt or raita as accompaniment to these main dishes, on Tuesday I will do dhansak (pg 102), beans with coconut (pg 154) and serve these with rice and salad. Because I also delight in European, Mediterranean and other such cuisines, they feature greatly in our weekly meals.

As for parties and special events, my brain starts to chart the meal to the minutest detail well before the event date. Numbers of people has a definite bearing on the dishes I select. For instance, for a large party I would refrain from doing koftas (pg 132) because this would involve a lot of time for preparations as well as for frying the koftas. This pre-planning for weekly meals and special event meals saves me a lot of time and money as it helps me do my shopping accordingly and in one go.

Finally, a typical well balanced vegetarian meal will comprise dal or beans, at least one vegetable, rice or bread (or both), fresh salad and yoghurt and other sundries such as pickle, chutney and papad. Such a meal will supply one with vitamins, minerals, proteins, carbohydrates and roughage, which are all so essential for healthy living.

Of course vegetarian meals can also be as unhealthy as one wants to make them, i.e.

a) if they are not nutritionally balanced, and b) if too much of butter, ghee, oil or spices are used in cooking. Normally in Indian cooking, these ingredients are used liberally only for special meals. Furthermore, generally sweets and puddings are not a part of the daily diet. Mostly fresh and dry fruits are eaten after a meal. Fresh fruits not only add to the balance of the diet but also help with the digestion of food.

The recipes in this book offer an extensive list of options when it comes to planning a menu. All the same I offer some suggestions here, keeping in mind that:

- *the mixture of dishes complement each other with regard to their taste and flavours*

- *the ingredients of each dish render it colour and texture which are then not repeated in another, in the same menu*

- *all the dishes in each menu are from the same region or regions where there is an overlap in style of cuisine.*

MENUS

Family Meal 1

Plain toor dal (pg 100), courgettes with garlic (pg 146), plain roti (pg 208),

plain rice (pg 201), plain yoghurt and fruit salad (pg 231)

Family Meal 2

Gujarati kaddhi (pg 86), green beans with potatoes (pg 153), Gujarati rotali (pg 210),

rice with ghee (pg 201), sambharo (pg 226)

Dinner Party 1

Starter: platter of pakoras (pg 48) sweet mint chutney (pg 243), tomato chutney (pg 246),

Main: kidney beans (pg 99), paneer in cream (pg 163), kofta (pg 132),

veg pulao (pg 203), plain roti (pg 208), pumpkin raita (pg 236), muli salad (pg 230),

Sweet: carrot halva (pg 258)

Dinner Party 2

Starter: batata wadda (pg 56), mixed salad chutney (pg 242),

mango or apple chutney (pg 244),

Main: sprouted moong (pg 96), tomato with coconut (pg 197), bhindi (pg 125),

plain rice (pg 201), plain puri (pg 221), koshambir (pg 227)

Sweet: shirkhand (pg 260)

Large Party Feast

Starter: moong dal bhajias (pg 50), coconut chutney 2 (pg 245),

hot coriander chutney (pg 242)

Main: black-eyed beans with bhindi (pg 71), paneer in tandoori masala (pg 164), bharta (pg 123),

cauliflower in garam masala (pg 138), fried rice (pg 202), missi roti (pg 212),

cucumber raita (pg 235), mixed salad (pg 227)

Sweet: barfi with almonds (pg 266), date and nut roll 1 (pg 268)

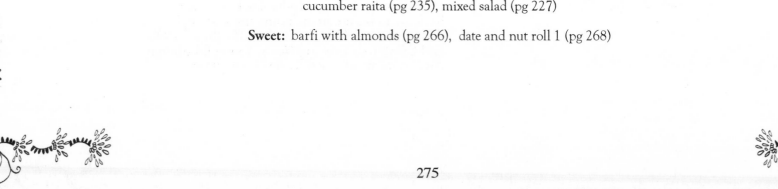

The Author

Mridu Shailaj Thanki was born in India but spent most of her adult life in the UK bringing up two children and working in the public and voluntary sector at a senior level. Her passion for cooking goes back to her childhood. She is skilful in producing cuisine from many cultures to a high standard. She has long standing experience of running cookery classes in different parts of the world and cooking for large groups and catering at festivals. She has also co-authored a previous book 'Our Lives and Hopes: Beyond Statistics and Reports', with Jyoti Dhingra, on the struggles and views of children living in the slums of Dhaka.

The Illustrator

Sandra de Matos is a French-Portuguese illustrator based in Edinburgh. After graduating from the Edinburgh College of Art, she has been involved in a number of projects and commissions, including picture books and printmaking. This cooking book has allowed Sandra to further her interest in Folk Art, drawing inspiration from Maddhubani painting for her illustrations.

The Graphic Designer

Calum Ross (b. 1988) is an Edinburgh born freelance designer with a BA (Hons) in Visual Communication. Since graduating from Edinburgh College of Art in 2009 he has attended Central Saint Martins University of the Arts in London and has had several commissions working on a variety of different projects from book to website design, contributing to Jotta Magazine and producing marketing materials for a variety of clients.

The Creative Avisor

Sushil Mangaonkar (b. 1972) is an artist/designer based in Edinburgh. He has done his MA in Fine Arts from Edinburgh and Mumbai. He specializes in drawing, painting, screen printing and photography and has handled several methods and modes of artistic expression. He has exhibited his work in solo as well as group exhibitions in UK and India. He has several honours to his credit including the National Award of the Lalit Kala Akademi, Delhi for 1998 and Edinburgh Evening News, Young Edinburgh Awards for youth friendly service in 2006.

By Leaves Entwined

I shall go down to this plot then
and see how things fare at ground level --
potatoes in rows, poppy and mint as and when
-- and take heart seeing artichoke revel.

With orange ladybirds from overseas
it will never be the same again,
and runner beans meshed in nasturtium leaves
stretching up and over in their joint yen.

And I shall think of my Indian bidie-in
who from curving pulses and shaping greens
will lovingly conjure with cardamom and cumin
such sense soaring meals – and some in-betweens.

Gordon Peters

NOTE

NOTE